Lowell's
Early Poems.

T. Y. CROWELL & Co.
NEW YORK

THE EARLY POEMS

OF

JAMES RUSSELL LOWELL.

WITH

BIOGRAPHICAL SKETCH

BY

NATHAN HASKELL DOLE.

———

NEW YORK: 46 East 14th Street.

THOMAS Y. CROWELL & COMPANY.

BOSTON: 100 Purchase Street.

CONTENTS.

CONTENTS.

JAMES RUSSELL LOWELL.

***

BIOGRAPHICAL SKETCH.

In the year 1639 Percival Lowle, or Lowell, a merchant of Bristol, England, landed at the little seaport town of Newbury, Mass.

We generally speak of a man's descent. In the case of James Russell Lowell's ancestry it was rather an ascent through eight generations. Percival Lowle's son, John L. Lowell, was a worthy cooper in old Newbury; his great-grandson was a shoemaker, his great-great-grandson was the Rev. John Lowell of Newburyport, who was the father of the Hon. John Lowell, by some regarded as the author of the clause in the Massachusetts Constitution abolishing slavery.

Judge Lowell's son, Charles, was a Unitarian minister, "learned, saintly, and discreet." He married Miss Harriet Traill Spence of Portsmouth, — a woman of superior mind, of great wit, vivacity, and an impetuosity that reached eccentricity. She was of Keltic blood, of a family that came from the Orkneys, and claimed descent from the Sir Patrick Spens of "the grand old ballad." Several of her family were connected with the American navy. Her father was Keith Spence, purser of the frigate "Philadelphia," and a prisoner at Tripoli.

By ancestry on both sides, and by connections with the Russells and other distinguished families, Lowell was the best type of the New England gentleman.

He was born on the 22d of February, 1819, at Elmwood, on Brattle Street, Cambridge.

This three-storied colonial mansion of wood was built in 1767 by Thomas Oliver, the last royal Lieutenant-Governor, before the Revolution.[1] Like other houses in "Tory Row," it was abandoned by its owners. Soon afterwards it came into possession of Elbridge Gerry, Governor of Massachusetts, and fifth Vice-President of the United States, whose memory and name are kept alive by the term "*Gerrymander.*" It next became the property of Dr. Lowell, about a year before the birth of his youngest child, and it was the home of the poet until his death.

Lowell's early education was obtained mainly at a school

---

[1] Thomas Oliver was graduated from Harvard College in the class of 1753. He was a gentleman of fortune, and lived first in Roxbury. He bought the property on Elmwood Avenue in 1766. When he accepted the royal commission of Lieutenant-Governor, he became President of the Council appointed by the King. On Sept. 2, 1774, about four thousand Middlesex freeholders assembled at Cambridge and compelled the mandamus councillors to resign. The President of the Council urged the propriety of delay, but the Committee would not spare him. He was forced to sign an agreement, "as a man of honor and a Christian, that he would never hereafter, upon any terms whatsoever, accept a seat at said Board on the present novel and oppressive form of government." He immediately quitted Cambridge; and when the British troops evacuated Boston he accompanied them. By an odd coincidence he went to reside at Bristol, England, where he died at the age of eighty-two years, in 1815, shortly before the Lowells, who were of Bristol origin, took possession of his former home. In Underwood's Sketch of Lowell, Thomas Oliver is confused with Chief Justice Peter Oliver, a man of a very different type of character.

kept nearly opposite Elmwood by a retired publisher, an Englishman, named William Wells. He also studied in the classical school of Mr. Daniel G. Ingraham in Boston. He was graduated from Harvard College in the class of 1838. Francis H. Underwood quotes him as frequently declaring that he read almost everything except the class-books prescribed by the faculty. Lowell says, in one of his early poems referring to Harvard, —

> " Tho lightly prized the ribboned parchments three,
>   Yet, *collegisse juvat*, I am glad
>   That here what colleging was mine I had."

He was secretary of the Hasty Pudding Society, and one of the editors of the short-lived college periodical *Harvardiana*, to which he contributed various articles in prose and verse. A serious escapade, which augured ill for his success in life, resulted in his suspension just before commencement in 1838. He had been elected poet of his class. This misfortune prevented him from delivering the poem which was afterwards published anonymously for private distribution. It contained a satire on aboli-tionists and reformers. He was sent for his own reform to Concord, where he resided in the family of Barzillai Frost, and made the acquaintance of Emerson, then begin-ning to rouse the ire of conservative Unitarianism by his transcendental philosophy, the brilliant but overestimated Margaret Fuller, who afterwards severely criticised his verse, and other well-known residents of the pretty town.

On his return to Cambridge he took up the study of law, and, in 1840, received the degree of LL.B. He even went so far as to open an office in Boston; but it is a question whether there was any actual basis of fact in a whimsical sketch of his entitled "My First Client," published in the short-lived *Boston Miscellany*, edited by Nathan Hale.

Several things engrossed Lowell's attention to the exclusion of law. Society at Cambridge was particularly attractive at that time. Allston the painter was living at Cambridgeport. Judge Story's pleasant home was on Brattle Street. The Fays then occupied the house which has since become the seat of "the Annex." Longfellow, described as "a slender, blond young professor," was established in the Craigie House. The famous names of Dr. Palfrey, Professor Andrews Norton, father of Lowell's friend and biographer, the "saintly" Henry Ware, and others will occur to the reader. With Emerson, Wyman, Agassiz, and Stillman, Lowell took long walks and excursions. He knew every inch of the beautiful ground then called "Sweet Auburn," now turned by the hand of misguided man into that most distressing of monstrosities — a modern cemetery. He haunted the poetic shades of the Waverley Oaks, heard the charming music of Beaver Brook, and climbed the hills of Belmont and Arlington. He penetrated the wild fastnesses of the Adirondacks, and fished in the clear waters of Moosehead Lake. Descriptions of these trips he contributed to the various periodicals which were then constantly springing up and dying after one or two issues.

He himself took his turn in establishing a magazine. In January, 1843, he started *The Pioneer*, to which Hawthorne, John Neal, Miss Barrett, Poe, Whittier, Story, Parsons, and others contributed, and which, in spite of such an array of talent, perished untimely during the winds of March.

He had already published, in 1841, a little volume of poems entitled "A Year's Life." They were marked by no great originality, betrayed little promise of future eminence, and Margaret Fuller, who reviewed them, was quite right in asserting that "neither the imagery nor the music of Lowell's verses was his own." The first sonnet in the present volume (page 31) practically acknowledges the force of this criticism. Lowell's later and correcter taste omitted most of them from his collected works.

Not far from Elmwood, but in the adjoining village of Watertown, lived one of Lowell's classmates, named White, whose sister, Maria, a slender, delicate girl, with a poetic genius in some respects more regulated and lofty than his own, early inspired him with a true and saving love. Speaking of the influences that moulded his life, George William Curtis says: —

"The first and most enduring was an early and happy passion for a lovely and high-minded woman who became his wife — the Egeria who exalted his youth and confirmed his noblest aspirations; a heaven-eyed counsellor of the serener air, who filled his mind with peace and his life with joy."

The young lady's prudent father objected to the marriage until the newly-fledged lawyer should be in a position to support a wife.

Shortly after the shipwreck of *The Pioneer*, Lowell was offered a hundred dollars by *Graham's Monthly* for ten poems. When Pegasus is able to earn such princely sums, there seems no reason why Love should be kept waiting at the cottage door. In 1844 Lowell published a new edition of his poems, and married Miss White. It was her influence that decided him to cast in his lot with the abolitionists. It was her refined taste that shaped and tempered his impetuous verse. A volume of her poems was afterwards privately printed, and is now very rare. It is an odd circumstance that in Lowell's library, from which Harvard College was allowed to select any volumes not in Gore Hall, neither this book nor any of Lowell's own early poems was to be found.

The young couple took up their residence at Elmwood, and here were born two daughters. One died early; the other still survives.

In 1845 appeared "The Vision of Sir Launfal," — a genuine inspiration composed in two days in a sort of ecstasy of poetic fervor. That more than anything established his fame. He recognized that he was dedicated to the Muses.

In 1846 he wrote: —

"If I have any vocation, it is the making of verse. When I take my pen for that, the world opens itself ungrudgingly before me; everything seems clear and easy, as it seems sinking to the bottom could be as one leans over the edge of his boat in one of those dear coves at Fresh Pond. . . . My true place is to serve the cause as a poet. Then my heart leaps before me into the conflict."

This year he began his "Biglow Papers" in the Boston *Courier*. Such *jeux d'esprit* are apt to be ephemeral. Lowell's are immortal. They have preserved in literary form a fast-fading dialect; they have caught and embalmed the mighty issues of a tremendous world-problem. Their influence was incalculable. He gathered them into a volume in 1848, and that same year became corresponding editor of the *Anti-Slavery Standard*. Fortunate man who throws himself into an unpopular cause which is in harmony with the Right! How different from Wordsworth, who attacked the ballot and took sides against reform!

Lowell's penchant for satire was exemplified again the same year in his "Fable for Critics" with its rhyming title-page:

> "A glance at a Few of our Literary Progenies
> (*Mrs. Malaprop's word*) from the Tub of Diogenes,
> Set forth in October, the 31st Day
> In the year '48, G. P. Putnam, Broadway."

In this Lowell with no sparing hand laid on his portraits most droll and amusing colors. It is a comic portrait gallery, a series of caricatures whose greatest value (as in all good caricatures) lies in the accurate presentation of characteristic features. He did not spare himself: —

> "There is Lowell, who's striving Parnassus to climb
> With a whole bale of *isms* tied together with rhyme.
> He might get on alone, spite of troubles and bowlders,
> But he can't with that bundle he has on his shoulders.
> The top of the hill he will ne'er come nigh reaching
> Till he learns the distinction 'twixt singing and preaching;
> His lyre has some chords that would ring pretty well,
> But he'd rather by half make a drum of the shell,
> And rattle away till he's old as Methusalem
> At the head of a march to the last New Jerusalem."

Some of his thrusts left embittered feelings, but in general the tone was so good-natured that only the thin-skinned could object, and it must be confessed many of his judgments have been confirmed by Time.

In 1851 Lowell visited Europe, and spent upwards of a year widening his acquaintance with the polite languages. But it is remarkable that Lowell gave the world almost no metrical translations. Shortly after his return his wife died (Oct. 27, 1853) in a slow decline. In reference to this bereavement Longfellow wrote his beautiful poem, "The Two Angels."

The following year Longfellow resigned his chair of Smith Professor of the French and Spanish Languages and Literature and Belles Lettres, and Lowell was appointed his successor with two years' leave of absence. He had won his spurs. He had collected his poems in two volumes, not including "A Year's Life," the "Biglow Papers," or the "Fable for Critics." He was known as one of the most brilliant contributors to *Putnam's Monthly* and other magazines.

In 1854 he delivered a series of twelve lectures on English poetry before the Lowell Institute. Ten years before he had published a volume of "Conversations on the Poets." The contrast between the two works was no less pronounced than that between his earlier and later poems.

In each, however, there is a tropical abundance which is confusing — Metaphors trample on the heels of Similes, and quaint and often grotesque conceits sometimes pall upon the taste, just as in the poems a flash of incongruous wit often disturbs the serenity that is desirable.

On his return from Europe, Mr. Lowell occupied the chair which he adorned by his fame rather than his actual work. He lectured on Dante, Shakespeare, Chaucer, and Cervantes, and delighted his audiences. But he was prone to be late at his college exercises, and often forgot them altogether.

Absence of mind was one of his characteristics. In connection with his professorship he became editor of the *Atlantic Monthly* in 1857. From 1863 until 1872 he was associated with Professor Charles Eliot Norton in the conduct of the *North American Review.* But he had a curious and annoying habit of carrying home manuscripts to read and then forgetting, or mislaying, or even losing them. As an editor he was not a brilliant success.

In 1857 he married Miss Frances Dunlap of Portland, Me., a cultivated lady who had been the governess of his daughter. She had unerring taste and sound judgment, and Mr. Lowell soon came to entrust to her the management of his financial affairs. She was enabled to make their comparatively small income more than meet the exigencies of an exacting position.

The second series of the "Biglow Papers," relating to the War of the Rebellion, were first published in the *Atlantic.* They were collected into a volume in 1865. That year was rendered notable by his "Commemoration Ode," the worthy crowning of one of the grandest poetic opportunities ever granted to man. "Under the Willows" appeared in 1869 ; "The Cathedral" in 1870.

In 1864 he had issued a collection of his early descriptive articles under the title, "Fireside Travels." In 1870 came "Among my Books." The second series followed in 1876. "My Study Windows" was published in 1871. All these prose works were marked by an exuberant, vivid, poetic, impassioned style. The tropical efflorescence of imagery was characteristic of them all. He ought to have remembered his own epigram, —

"Over-ornament ruins both poem and prose."

In 1876 appeared three memorial poems: that read at Concord, April 19, 1875; that read at Cambridge under the Washington Elm, July 3, 1875; and the Fourth of July Ode of 1876. This year Mr. Lowell was appointed one of the presidential electors; and the following year President Hayes first offered him the Austrian mission, and, on his refusal of that, gave him the honorary post at Madrid, which had been adorned by Everett, Irving, and Prescott. He was there three years, and, on the retirement of Mr. Welsh in 1880, he was transferred to the Court of St. James, or, as one of the English papers expressed it, he became "His Excellency the Ambassador of American Literature to the Court of Shakespeare."

He was extremely popular. Known in private as "one of the most marvellous of story-tellers," he became the lion of all public occasions. The *London News* spoke of the "Extraordinary felicity of his occasional speeches." At Birmingham he delivered a noble address on Democracy. He was selected to deliver the oration at the dedication of the Dean Stanley Memorial. He spoke on Fielding at Taunton, on Coleridge at Westminster Abbey, on Gray at Cambridge.

He was President of the Wordsworth Society. All sorts of honors were heaped upon him, both at home and abroad.

He returned to America in 1885, and once more occupied the somewhat dilapidated mansion at Elmwood. Once more he moved amid his rare and precious books, and heard the birds singing in the elms which his father had planted, or in the clustered bushes back of the house. He took a deep interest in the struggle for international copyright. He was President of the American League, and wrote the memorable lines:—

> "In vain we call old notions fudge,
>   And bend our conscience to our dealing;
> The Ten Commandments will not budge;
>   And stealing *will* continue stealing."

He occupied the leisure of his failing health in revising his works. His last volume of poems was entitled "Heart's Ease and Rue." One of his latest poems "My Book," appeared in the Christmas number of the New York *Ledger* in 1890. In the December number of the *Atlantic* his hand was visible in the anonymous "Contributor's Club." His very last poem is believed to be the inscription for a memorial bust of Fielding.

During the last years his health was a matter of grave anxiety to his friends. In the spring of 1891 he seemed better. He was engaged in writing a life of Nathaniel Hawthorne. When the present writer called to see him one beautiful spring day, he found him in his library, at that moment engaged in making suggestions for the inscriptions on the new Boston Public Library. His manner was the perfection of courtesy and high breeding. His keen eyes seemed to read the very soul. The slight affectation of English speech which drew upon him some criticism, was not evinced in private conversation, nor did the use of the little word "I" appear unduly, as in some of his occasional speeches. Simplicity and beautiful dignity, tempered by evident feebleness of health, made him a memorable figure.

Toward the end of the summer he suddenly grew more

seriously ill. He suffered severely, and his last words were, "Oh! why don't you let me die?"

He drew his last breath in the early morning of Aug. 12, 1891. He was buried at Mount Auburn, in the shadow of Indian Ridge, not far from Longfellow's grave, in a lot unenclosed and marked by no monument.

Memorial services were held at Westminster Abbey and elsewhere. Lord Tennyson cabled a message of sympathy: "England and America will mourn Mr. Lowell's death. They loved him and he loved them." The Queen publicly expressed her respect and sorrow.

Few men have left a deeper impress on their age. Few men have used noble powers more nobly. In private life and public station there is not a shadow to stain the whiteness of his fame.

As a poet he stands in the front rank of those who have yet appeared in America. As a critic he was generous and just; as a humorist he used his shafts of ridicule only to wound wrong; as a statesman and diplomat he was actuated by broad, far-seeing views; as a man he was a type to be upheld and followed. America has just cause to reverence his memory; and the whole English-speaking world, without geographical distinction, claim him as their own.

NATHAN HASKELL DOLE.

A LEGEND OF BRITTANY.

PART FIRST.

I.

FAIR as a summer dream was Margaret, —
  Such dream as in a poet's soul might start,
Musing of old loves while the moon doth set:
  Her hair was not more sunny than her heart,
Though like a natural golden coronet
  It circled her dear head with careless art,
Mocking the sunshine, that would fain have lent
To its frank grace a richer ornament.

II.

His loved-one's eyes could poet ever speak,
  So kind, so dewy, and so deep were hers, —
But, while he strives, the choicest phrase, too weak,
  Their glad reflection in his spirit blurs;
As one may see a dream dissolve and break
  Out of his grasp when he to tell it stirs,
Like that sad Dryad doomed no more to bless
The mortal who revealed her loveliness.

III.

She dwelt forever in a region bright,
    Peopled with living fancies of her own,
Where naught could come but visions of delight,
    Far, far aloof from earth's eternal moan:
A summer cloud thrilled through with rosy light,
    Floating beneath the blue sky all alone,
Her spirit wandered by itself, and won
A golden edge from some unsetting sun.

IV.

The heart grows richer that its lot is poor, —
    God blesses want with larger sympathies, —
Love enters gladliest at the humble door,
    And makes the cot a palace with his eyes; —
So Margaret's heart a softer beauty wore,
    And grew in gentleness and patience wise,
For she was but a simple herdsman's child,
A lily chance-sown in the rugged wild.

V.

There was no beauty of the wood or field
    But she its fragrant bosom-secret knew,
Nor any but to her would freely yield
    Some grace that in her soul took root and grew:
Nature to her glowed ever new-revealed,
    All rosy-fresh with innocent morning dew,
And looked into her heart with dim, sweet eyes
That left it full of sylvan memories.

VI.

O, what a face was hers to brighten light,
   And give back sunshine with an added glow,
To wile each moment with a fresh delight,
   And part of memory's best contentment grow!
O, how her voice, as with an inmate's right,
   Into the strangest heart would welcome go,
And make it sweet, and ready to become
Of white and gracious thoughts the chosen home!

VII.

None looked upon her but he straightway thought
   Of all the greenest depths of country cheer,
And into each one's heart was freshly brought
   What was to him the sweetest time of year,
So was her every look and motion fraught
   With out-of-door delights and forest lere;
Not the first violet on a woodland lea
Seemed a more visible gift of spring than she.

VIII.

Is love learned only out of poets' books?
   Is there not somewhat in the dropping flood,
And in the nunneries of silent nooks,
   And in the murmured longing of the wood,
That could make Margaret dream of lovelorn looks,
   And stir a thrilling mystery in her blood
More trembly secret than Aurora's tear
Shed in the bosom of an eglatere?

IX.

Full many a sweet forewarning hath the mind,
    Full many a whispering of vague desire,
Ere comes the nature destined to unbind
    Its virgin zone, and all its deeps inspire, —
Low stirrings in the leaves, before the wind
    Wakes all the green strings of the forest lyre,
Faint heatings in the calyx, ere the rose
Its warm, voluptuous breast doth all unclose.

X.

Long in its dim recesses pines the spirit,
    Wildered and dark, despairingly alone;
Though many a shape of beauty wander near it,
    And many a wild and half-remembered tone
Tremble from the divine abyss to cheer it,
    Yet still it knows that there is only one
Before whom it can kneel and tribute bring,
Yet be far less a vassal than a king.

XI.

To feel a want, yet scarce know what it is,
    To seek one nature that is always new,
Whose glance is warmer than another's kiss,
    Whom we can bare our inmost beauty to
Nor feel deserted afterwards, — for this
    But with our destined comate we can do, —
Such longing instinct fills the mighty scope
Of the young soul with one mysterious hope.

XII.

Naught as a maiden's soul is bountiful,
    For beauty's law is bounty : it must be
That, when the heart with blessedness is full,
    It droops into a sated apathy,
Unless the choice blooms of that bliss it cull
    To crown another with, and make it free
Of beauty's harvest, which unfruitful lies,
Wanting the ripening light of loving eyes.

XIII.

So Margaret's heart grew brimming with the lore
    Of love's enticing secrets ; and although
She had found none to cast it down before,
    Yet oft to Fancy's chapel she would go
To pay her vows, and count the rosary o'er
    Of her love's promised graces : — haply so
Miranda's hope had pictured Ferdinand
Long ere the gaunt wave tossed him on the strand.

XIV.

A new-made star that swims the lonely gloom,
    Unwedded yet and longing for the sun,
Whose beams, the bride-gifts of the lavish groom,
    Blithely to crown the virgin planet run,
Her being was, watching to see the bloom
    Of love's fresh sunrise roofing one by one
Its clouds with gold, a triumph-arch to be
For him who came to hold her heart in fee.

XV.

Her sun arose to redden in eclipse,
    Alas! too soon, ere yet 't was risen wholly, —
But let us not unseal the morrow's lips;
    Swiftly enough thou comest, Melancholy,
And what we win of earth's contentment slips
    From our forlorn embraces not too slowly:
Let the bright mist of morning cover now
From our pleased eyes the future's sullen brow.

XVI.

Not far from Margaret's cottage dwelt a knight
    Of the proud Templars, a sworn celibate,
Whose heart in secret fed upon the light
    And dew of her ripe beauty, through the gate
Of his close vow catching what gleams he might
    Of the free heaven, and cursing — all too late —
The cruel faith whose black walls hemmed him in
And turned life's crowning bliss to deadly sin,

XVII.

For he had met her in the wood by chance,
    And, having drunk her beauty's wildering spell,
His heart shook like the pennon of a lance
    That quivers in a breeze's sudden swell,
And thenceforth, in a close enfolded trance,
    From mistily golden deep to deep he fell;
The earth did waver and fade far away
Beneath the hope in whose warm arms he lay

XVIII.

A dark, proud man he was, whose half-blown youth
   Had shed its blossoms even in opening,
Leaving a few that with more winning ruth
   Trembling around grave manhood's stem might
      cling,
More sad than cheery, making, in good sooth,
   Like the fringed gentian, a late autumn spring:—
A twilight nature, braided light and gloom,
A youth half-smiling by an open tomb.

XIX.

Fair as an angel, who yet inly wore
   A wrinkled heart foreboding his near fall;
Who saw him alway wished to know him more,
   As if he were some fate's defiant thrall
And nursed a dreaded secret at his core;
   Little he loved, but power most of all,
And that he seemed to scorn, as one who knew
By what foul paths men choose to crawl thereto.

XX.

Yet by long sufferance this love had grown
   Into a passion with him, that would make
As great a triumph for a child o'erthrown
   As for a giant, and, self-blinded, take
Ambition's meanest footstool for a throne:
   So day by day he nursed a bitterer ache
At heart, and learned to see no wider realm
Than could be spanned by a grand-master's helm.

XXI.

He could seem noble a rich end to gain,
  And he would talk of nobleness, as 't were
A gift as cheap and common as the rain;
  Praise was a thing it seemed he could not bear,
Wrapping himself therefrom in high disdain,
  Yet his most careless deeds were done with care,
And, if they were unheeded or unseen,
A passing shade of gall would cloud his mien.

XXII.

He had been noble, but some great deceit
  Had turned his better instinct to a vice:
He strove to think the world was all a cheat,
  That power and fame were cheap at any price,
That the sure way of being shortly great
  Was even to play life's game with loaded dice,
Since he had tried the honest play and found
That vice and virtue differed but in sound.

XXIII.

But none can wholly put his heart away,
  And, though he aimed to act upon a plan
Of steady fraud to keep his soul at bay,
  Yet sometimes through his breast an instinct ran,
That roused the memory of a purer day
  Ere life to be a bitter toil began:
A self-made minotaur, half man half beast,
He bound himself and longed to be released.

XXIV.

Spurn at the world and it will deem you great,
　Scorn it if you would win its high esteem,
Make your own chance, life is too short to wait
　Until the side of error kicks the beam,
Set down your value at your own huge rate,
　The world will pay it ; — such was his weak scheme
To make the most of life, and it serves well
Those who would go no deeper than the shell.

XXV.

Yet Margaret's sight redeemed him for a space
　From his own thraldom ; man could never be
A hypocrite when first such maiden grace
　Smiled in upon his heart ; the agony
Of wearing all day long a lying face
　Fell lightly from him, and, a moment free,
Erect with wakened faith in spirit stood
And scorned the weakness of its demon-mood.

XXVI.

Like a sweet wind-harp to him was her thought,
　Which would not let the common air come near,
Till from its dim enchantment it had caught
　A musical tenderness that brimmed his ear
With sweetness more ethereal than aught
　Save silver-dropping snatches that whilere
Rained down from some sad angel's faithful harp
To cool her fallen lover's anguish sharp.

XXVII.

Deep in the forest was a little dell
  High overarched with the leafy sweep
Of a broad oak, through whose gnarled roots there fell
  A slender rill that sung itself asleep,
Where its continuous toil had scooped a well
  To please the fairy folk ; breathlessly deep
The stillness was, save when the dreaming brook
From its small urn a drizzly murmur shook.

XXVIII.

The wooded hills sloped upward all around
  With gradual rise, and made an even rim,
So that it seemed a mighty casque unbound
  From some huge Titan's brow to lighten him,
Ages ago, and left upon the ground,
  Where the slow soil had mossed it to the brim,
Till after countless centuries it grew
Into this dell, the haunt of noontide dew.

XXIX.

Dim vistas, sprinkled o'er with sun-flecked green,
  Wound through the thickset trunks on every side,
And, toward the west, in fancy may be seen
  A gothic window in its blazing pride,
When the low sun, two arching elms between,
  Lit up the leaves beyond, which, autumn-dyed
With lavish hues, would into splendor start,
Shaming the labored panes of richest art.

XXX.

Here, leaning once against the old oak's trunk,
  Mordred, for such was the young Templar's name,
Saw Margaret come; unseen, the falcon shrunk
  From the meek dove; sharp thrills of tingling flame
Made him forget that he was vowed a monk,
  And all the outworks of his pride o'ercame :
Flooded he seemed with bright delicious pain,
As if a star had burst within his brain.

XXXI

Such power hath beauty and frank innocence:
  A flower burst forth, that sunshine glad to bless,
Even from his love's long leafless stem; the sense
  Of exile from Hope's happy realm grew less,
And thoughts of childish peace, he knew not whence,
  Thronged round his heart with many an old caress,
Melting the frost there into pearly dew
That mirrored back his nature's morning-blue.

XXXII.

She turned and saw him, but she felt no dread,
  Her purity, like adamantine mail,
Did so encircle her; and yet her head
  She drooped, and made her golden hair her veil,
Through which a glow of rosiest lustre spread,
  Then faded, and anon she stood all pale,
As snow o'er which a blush of northern-light
Suddenly reddens, and as soon grows white.

XXXIII.

She thought of Tristrem and of Lancilot,
  Of all her dreams, and of kind fairies' might,
And how that dell was deemed a haunted spot,
  Until there grew a mist before her sight,
And where the present was she half forgot,
  Borne backward through the realms of old
    delight, —
Then, starting up awake, she would have gone,
Yet almost wished it might not be alone

XXXIV.

How they went home together through the wood,
  And how all life seemed focused into one
Thought-dazzling spot that set ablaze the blood,
  What need to tell? Fit language there is none
For the heart's deepest things.   Who ever wooed
  As in his boyish hope he would have done?
For, when the soul is fullest, the hushed tongue
Voicelessly trembles like a lute unstrung.

XXXV.

But all things carry the heart's messages
  And know it not, nor doth the heart well know,
But nature hath her will; even as the bees,
  Blithe go-betweens, fly singing to and fro
With the fruit-quickening pollen; — hard if these
  Found not some all unthought-of way to show
Their secret each to each; and so they did,
And one heart's flower-dust into the other slid.

XXXVI.

Young hearts are free; the selfish world it is
  That turns them miserly and cold as stone,
And makes them clutch their fingers on the bliss,
  Which but in giving truly is their own; —
She had no dreams of barter, asked not his,
  But gave hers freely as she would have thrown
A rose to him, or as that rose gives forth
Its generous fragrance, thoughtless of its worth.

XXXVII.

We only prize those hearts that do not prize
  Themselves: love by its nature shrinks
From any thought of grovelling merchandise,
  And, like a humming bird a-wing, it drinks
From flowerlike souls the honeydew that lies
  Wide open to the air, and never thinks
Of its own worth or theirs, or aught beside
But joy and sunlight and life's morning tide.

XXXVIII.

Her summer nature felt a need to bless,
  And a like longing to be blest again;
So, from her skylight spirit, gentleness
  Dropt ever like a sunlit fall of rain,
And his beneath drank in the bright caress
  As thirstily as would a parched plain,
That long hath watched the showers of sloping gray
For ever, ever, falling far away.

XXXIX.

Now Margaret hath gained her secret bower,
   Where musing she gazed up into the blue
Calm heaven, which looked as it could never lower,
   Now that her happy dreams had come so true:
Life seemed the birth of that last crowded hour,
   And, all impearled with sunshine and fresh dew,
It lay before her like a summer walk,
An hour of trembling looks and ravished talk.

XL.

O, might life fade away and gently cease
   While the heart vibrates like a golden string,
Ending in music and forgetful peace,
   While untried hope is full of sinewy spring
As a new bow, ere yet by slow degrees
   Earth's dust hath clotted round the soul's fresh wing
And made us flutter, sink, and crawl, and die,
Heart-broken by our instinct for the sky!

XLI.

But Earth is Earth, and beautiful is she
   Our mother, from whose fertile breast we draw
Half of our nature: it is destiny
   That we flee to her from the gloomy maw
Of the unknown; for we can never see
   More than a fragment of the spirit's law,
And clasp her hand most closely when we might
Be weaned at once, and feed on nectarous light.

XLII.

Sorrow, there seemeth more of thee in life
　Than we can bear and live, and yet we bear;
And thy endurance is the desperate knife
　Wherewith the cable of our dreams we share,
To steer out boldly through the monstrous strife
　Of surging action, and learn how to dare,
And drive right onward through the grasping seas
To Will and Power, which give the soul true ease.

XLIII.

Yet let us dream while we are anchored yet,
　If so some portion of the destined ache
That haunts the spirit here we may forget:
　Who never dreamed is never well-awake;
The stars of life one after other set,
　And, while we can with faith, 't is good to make
The world seem what it was when first we turned
Saw its broad stretch, and for its triumphs burned.

XLIV.

Could Margaret have seen the shaft of woe
　Which fate even now was drawing to the head,
Even in the very twanging of the bow,
　Whose aim must strike her soaring gladness dead.
She would have shut her eyes upon the blow,
　And all her soul upon her lover shed,
Though life went with it, — so the heart is fain
To gamble present bliss for future pain.

XLV.

No matter, woe is short and life is long:
    We prate too much of this world's flitting grief,
Thoughtless of the unimaginable throng
    Of after-lives that bring the soul relief
And countless chances more: like oak-trees strong,
    We shed our frail lives from us, leaf by leaf,
And each new death but brings the spirit more
Broad worlds to win and beauty to adore.

XLVI.

So, Margaret, let thy heart leap up to hear,
    Each night, the rustle of the leaves which tells
That the long dreamed-of ecstasy is near,
    That made the day seem empty: O, what swells
Of brightly mingled, sudden hope and fear
    Hast thou, awaiting him since curfew bells
Have died away, and Hesper in the west
Trembled as doth the joy within thy breast!

XLVII.

How should she dream of ill? the heart filled quite
    With sunshine, like the shepherd's-clock at noon,
Closes its leaves around its warm delight;
    Whate'er in life is harsh or out of tune
Is all shut out, no boding shade of blight
    Can pierce the opiate ether of its swoon:
Love is but blind as thoughtful justice is,
But naught can be so wanton-blind as bliss.

XLVIII.

When Mordred came, all soul she seemed to be,
  And quite broke through the clay's entangling
    mesh,
His spirit with her eyes she seemed to see,
  And feel its motion in her very flesh;
And, when he went, his radiant memory
  Robed all her fantasies with glory fresh,
As if an angel, quitting her awhile,
Left round her heart the halo of his smile.

XLIX.

Bright passion of young hearts, like the huge burst
  Of some grand symphony all unaware
Storming the soul, majestic as the first
  Sight of the rousing ocean, — poor and bare,
And barren of all life as spots accurst,
  Thou mak'st all other joys, once deemed most rare!
So Margaret thought when Mordred went away
And made day night, or came and made night day.

L.

All beauty and all life he was to her;
  She questioned not his love, she only knew
That she loved him, and not a pulse could stir
  In her whole frame but quivered through and
    through
With this glad thought, and was a minister
  To do him fealty and service true,
Like golden ripples hasting to the land
To wreck their freight of sunshine on the strand.

LI.

O dewy dawn of love! O hopes that are
    Hung high, like the cliff-swallow's perilous nest,
Most like to fall when fullest, and that jar
    With every heavier billow! O unrest
Than balmiest deeps of quiet sweeter far!
    How did ye triumph now in Margaret's breast,
Making it readier to shrink and start
Than the pond-lily's golden quivering heart!

LII.

Here let us pause: O, would the soul might ever
    Achieve its immortality in youth,
When nothing yet hath damped its high endeavor
    After the starry energy of truth!
Here let us pause, and for a moment sever
    This gleam of sunshine from the days unruth
That sometime come to all, for it is good
To lengthen to the last a sunny mood.

LIII.

Hope skims o'er life as we may sometimes see
    A butterfly, whose home is in the flowers,
Blown outward far over the moaning sea,
    Remembering in vain its odorous bowers;
It flutters o'er the drear immensity
    To sink ere long: there are not many hours
Ere the heart wonders at the simple hope
That danced so gayly forth with fate to cope.

LIV.

But Faith comes ever after Hope is fled,
   Hope's ghost, with sadder yet with fairer face,
To tell us that she is but seeming dead;
   That earth is but her body's burial-place,
Whence flowers shall spring, on lowly hearts to shed
   A fragrant prophecy of heaven's grace,
And that we truly could not see her, even,
Till she had flitted to her home in heaven.

A LEGEND OF BRITTANY.

PART SECOND.

I.

As one who, from the sunshine and the green,
   Enters the solid darkness of a cave,
Nor knows what precipice or pit unseen
   May yawn before him with its sudden grave,
And, with hushed breath, doth often forward lean,
   Deeming he hears the plashing of a wave
Dimly below, or feels a damper air
From out some dreary chasm, he knows not where ; —

II.

So, from the sunshine and the green of love,
   We enter on our story's darker part ;
And, though the horror of it well may move
   An impulse of repugnance in the heart,
Yet let us think, that, as there 's naught above
   The all-embracing atmosphere of Art,
So also there is naught that falls below
Her generous reach, though grimed with guilt and
     woe.

III.

Her fittest triumph is to show that good
  Lurks in the heart of evil evermore,
That love, though scorned, and outcast, and with-
      stood,
  Can without end forgive, and yet have store;
God's love and man's are of the self-same blood,
  And He can see that always at the door
Of foulest hearts the angel-nature yet
Knocks to return and cancel all its debt.

IV.

It ever is weak falsehood's destiny
  That her thick mask turns crystal to let through
The unsuspicious eyes of honesty;
  But Margaret's heart was too sincere and true
Aught but plain truth and faithfulness to see,
  And Mordred's for a time a little grew
To be like hers, won by the mild reproof
Of those kind eyes that kept all doubt aloof.

V.

Full oft they met, as dawn and twilight meet
  In northern climes; she full of growing day,
As he of darkness, which before her feet
  Shrank gradual, and faded quite away,
Soon to return; for power made love sweet
  To him, and, when his will had gained full sway,
The taste began to pall; for never power
Can sate the hungry soul beyond an hour.

VI.

At first he loved her truly; its far goal
    His weary heart had reached and sunk to rest:
She seemed a white-browed angel sent to roll
    The heavy stone away which long had prest,
As in a living sepulchre, his soul:
    But soon the customed nature of his breast
Awoke, and in its iron hand once more
Shook the fierce lash that seared him to the core.

VII.

A healthy love of power thaws the ice
    Wherewith sloth fetters oft the gushing will;
But, when the soul lusts after it, no vice
    Is half so deadly; then it tries its skill
In heaping for its sin some monstrous price
    To make it precious; but, like morning, still
Comes the pale afterthought, and makes it see
The harlot whose poor slave it crouched to be.

VIII.

Such lust in Mordred's soul had dug its lair,
    Taking for ransom all good impulses:
Love might have saved him, which makes virtues rare
    Even of our vices, as, upon his knees,
Stout Kempion kissed the dragon thrice, and there
    Found in its stead the maiden, his heart's peace;
But he loved Margaret only for the power
It gave him o'er her heart, her virgin dower.

IX.

And, having gained it, still he craved for more;
　　Margaret could yield no more save innocence,
And this his thought would often hover o'er,
　　Poising to swoop, not for the glut of sense,
But to enjoy his mastery to the core,
　　And probe the depth of his bad influence;
Such hunger gnawed him and such fierce unrest,
As one who hath a serpent in his breast.

X.

He wrestled with his will, he felt the shame,
　　The crowning anguish, which the spirit feels
When a pure instinct flies to whence it came,
　　And in its place a slimy viper steals,
Lulling asleep our guardian sense of blame,
　　Till on its throne our better nature reels:
He felt the shame, the anguish, and the sin,
Yet oped his heart and let the foul thing in.

XI.

So to his will he won her by degrees,
　　Working upon her faith with secret wear,
Steadfast and silent as the tireless seas
　　Gain on the shore; his thirst he could not bear,
Once having drained love's beaker to the lees,
　　And, could he quench its flame, he felt no care
If he drank poison: so at last he fell,
Winning the crime he plotted for so well.

XII

He fell as doth the tempter ever fall,
   Even in the gaining of his loathsome end;
God doth not work as man works, but makes all
   The crooked paths of ill to goodness tend;
Let him judge Margaret! If to be the thrall
   Of love, and faith too generous to defend
Its very life from him she loved, be sin,
What hope of grace may the seducer win?

XIII.

Grim-hearted world, that look'st with Levite eyes
   On those poor fallen by too much faith in man,
She that upon thy freezing threshold lies,
   Starved to more sinning by thy savage ban, —
Seeking that refuge because foulest vice
   More godlike than thy virtue is, whose span
Shuts out the wretched only, — is more free
From all her crimes than thou wilt ever be!

XIV.

Thou wilt not let her wash thy dainty feet
   With such salt things as tears, or with rude hair
Dry them, soft Pharisee, that sit'st at meat
   With him who made her such, and speak'st him
      fair,
Leaving God's wandering lamb the while to bleat
   Unheeded, shivering in the pitiless air:
Thou hast made prisoned virtue show more wan
And haggard than a vice to look upon.

XV.

Now many months flew by, and weary grew
    To Margaret the sight of happy things;
Blight fell on all her flowers, instead of dew;
    Shut round her heart were now the joyous wings
Wherewith it wont to soar; yet not untrue,
    Though tempted much, her woman's nature clings
To its first pure belief, and with sad eyes
Looks backward o'er the gate of Paradise.

XVI.

Not wholly desolate, nor quite shut out
    From peace, are hearts that love, though hope-
            lessly;
Though, with rude billows compassed all about,
    They toss, lone shipwrecks, on a dreary sea,
Yet love hath glories which the eye of doubt
    Withers to look on, for he holds the key
Which opens in the soul that inner cell,
Where in deep peace the heavenly instincts dwell.

XVII.

So Margaret, though Mordred came less oft,
    And winter frowned where spring had laughed
            before,
In his strange eyes, yet half her sadness doffed,
    And in her silent patience loved him more:
Sorrow had made her soft heart yet more soft,
    And a new life within her own she bore
Which made her tenderer, as she felt it move
Beneath her breast, — a refuge for her love.

XVIII.

This babe, she thought, would surely bring him
        back,
    And be a bond forever them between;
Before its eyes the sullen tempest-rack
    Would fade, and leave the face of heaven serene;
And love's return doth more than fill the lack,
    Which in his absence withered the heart's green:
And yet a dim foreboding still would flit
Between her and her hope to darken it.

XIX.

She could not figure forth a happy fate,
    Even for this life from heaven so newly come;
The earth must needs be doubly desolate
    To him scarce parted from a fairer home:
Such boding heavier on her bosom sate
    One night, as, standing in the twilight gloam,
She strained her eyes beyond that dizzy verge
At whose foot faintly breaks the future's surge.

XX.

Poor little spirit! naught but shame and woe
    Nurse the sick heart whose lifeblood nurses thine:
Yet not those only; love hath triumphed so,
    As for thy sake makes sorrow more divine:
And yet, though thou be pure, the world is foe
    To purity, if born in such a shrine;
And, having trampled it for struggling thence,
Smiles to itself and calls it Providence.

XXI.

O mockery, that aught unruth and hard
  Behind God's name its ugly face should veil!
Sad human nature, that o'er flint and shard
  With bleeding feet shrink'st onward wan and pale,
Believing 't is thy doom to be ill-starred,
  Since e'en Religion sanctions the foul tale,
And hating God, because man's creeds but grant
What they his blessings call, — toil, woe, and want!

XXII.

As thus she mused, a shadow seemed to rise
  From out her thought, and turn to dreariness
All blissful hopes and sunny memories,
  And the quick blood doth curdle up and press
About her heart, which seemed to shut its eyes
  And hush itself, as who with shuddering guess
Harks through the gloom and dreads e'en now to feel
Through his hot breast the icy slide of steel.

XXIII.

But, at that heart-beat, while in dread she was,
  In the low wind the honeysuckles gleam,
A dewy thrill flits through the heavy grass,
  And, looking forth, she saw, as in a dream,
Within the wood the moonlight's shadowy mass:
  Night's starry heart yearning to hers doth seem,
And the deep sky, full-hearted with the moon,
Folds round her all the happiness of June.

XXIV.

What fear could face a heaven and earth like this?
   What silveriest cloud could hang 'neath such a
      sky?
A tide of wondrous and unwonted bliss
   Rolls back through all her pulses suddenly,
As if some seraph, who had learned to kiss
   From the fair daughters of the world gone by,
Has wedded so his fallen light with hers,
Such sweet, strange joy through soul and body stirs.

XXV.

So God leads back in silence those who err
   From noble promptings, to his hope again;
So gentle Nature plays the comforter
   To all who seek at man's proud door in vain:
And gladly once again awoke in her
   The peace that long in drowsy dark had lain,
And she could feel that hope is never flown,
That God ne'er leaves the soul to grope alone.

XXVI.

Now seek we Mordred: He who did not fear
   The crime, yet fears the latent consequence:
If it should reach a brother Templar's ear,
   It haply might be made a good pretence
To cheat him of the hope he held most dear;
   For he had spared no thought's or deed's expense,
That by and by might help his wish to clip
Its darling bride, — the high grand-mastership.

XXVII.

Upon his casement, with a knotted brow,
  He learned and mused ; dark shadows came and
      past
O'er his pale cheek ; some dreadful tempting now
  Coils round his heart, which struggles all aghast
And fain would shake it off, yet knows not how,
  Then struggles less and less, and yields at last,
And the black serpent, colder and more cold,
Half sleeps, but tightens still its scaly fold.

XXVIII.

The apathy, ere a crime resolved is done,
  Is scarce less dreadful than remorse for crime ;
By no allurement can the soul be won
  From brooding o'er the weary creep of time :
Mordred stole forth into the happy sun,
  Striving to hum a scrap of Breton rhyme,
But the sky struck him speechless, and he tried
In vain to summon up his callous pride.

XXIX.

In the court-yard a fountain leaped alway,
  A Triton blowing jewels through his shell
Into the sunshine ; Mordred turned away,
  Weary because the stone face did not tell
Of weariness, nor could he bear to-day,
  Heartsick, to hear the patient sink and swell
Of winds among the leaves, or golden bees
Drowsily humming in the orange-trees.

XXX.

All happy sights and sounds now came to him
    Like a reproach : he wandered far and wide,
Following the lead of his unquiet whim,
    But still there went a something at his side
That made the cool breeze hot, the sunshine dim ;
    It would not flee, it could not be defied,
He could not see it, but he felt it there
By the damp chill that crept among his hair.

XXXI.

Day wore at last ; the evening star arose,
    And throbbing in the sky grew red and set ;
Then with a guilty, wavering step he goes
    To the hid nook where they so oft had met
In happier season, for his heart well knows
    That he is sure to find poor Margaret
Watching and waiting there with lovelorn breast
Around her young dream's rudely scattered nest.

XXXII.

Swifter and paler than a sheeted ghost
    Out of the heavy darkness glimmereth
To tell some widowed heart that all is lost,
    He started close beside her with hard breath
And heavy, as of one long tempest-tost
    On the wild main of guilty thoughts, where death
And life strive for the spirit, not the clay,
And death's lean hand hath wellnigh clutched its prey.

XXXIII.

"Sweet Margaret!" he said, but in his tone
    A something froze her, as if duty tried
To mock the voice of love now long since flown,
    And made her feel, with Mordred at her side,
More palpably and bitterly alone :
    There stood they, she but doubly beautified
By her meek sadness and the moon's pale glow,
He seeming darker for that light to grow.

XXXIV.

Why follow here that grim old chronicle
    Which counts the dagger-strokes and drops of
        blood?
Enough that Margaret by his mad steel fell,
    Unmoved by murder from her trusting mood,
Smiling on him as Heaven smiles on Hell,
    With a sad love, remembering when he stood
Not fallen yet, the unsealer of her heart,
Of all her holy dreams the holiest part.

XXXV.

His crime complete, scarce knowing what he did,
    (So goes the tale,) beneath the altar there
In the high church the stiffening corpse he hid,
    And then, to 'scape that suffocating air,
Like a scared ghoule out of the porch he slid ;
    But his strained eyes saw bloodspots everywhere,
And ghastly faces thrust themselves between
His soul and hopes of peace with blasting mien.

XXXVI.

His heart went out within him, like a spark
　　Dropt in the sea; wherever he made bold
To turn his eyes, he saw, all stiff and stark,
　　Pale Margaret lying dead; the lavish gold
Of her loose hair seemed in the cloudy dark
　　To spread a glory, and a thousandfold
More strangely pale and beautiful she grew:
Her silence stabbed his conscience through and
　　　　through:

XXXVII.

Or visions of past days, — a mother's eyes
　　That smiled down on the fair boy at her knee,
Whose happy upturned face to hers replies, —
　　He saw sometimes; or Margaret mournfully
Gazed on him full of doubt, as one who tries
　　To crush belief that does love injury;
Then she would wring her hands, but soon again
Love's patience glimmered out through cloudy pain.

XXXVIII.

Meanwhile he dared not go and steal away
　　The silent, dead-cold witness of his sin;
He had not feared the life, but that dull clay,
　　Those open eyes that showed the death within,
Would surely stare him mad; yet all the day
　　A dreadful impulse, whence his will could win
No refuge, made him linger in the aisle,
Freezing with his wan look each greeting smile.

XXXIX.

Now, on the second day, there was to be
   A festival in church: from far and near
Came flocking in the sun-burnt peasantry,
   And knights and dames with stately antique cheer,
Blazing with pomp, as if all faërie
   Had emptied her quaint halls, or, as it were,
The illuminated marge of some old book,
While we were gazing, life and motion took.

XL.

When all were entered, and the roving eyes
   Of all were staid, some upon faces bright,
Some on the priests, some on the traceries
   That decked the slumber of a marble knight,
And all the rustlings over that arise
   From recognizing tokens of delight,
When friendly glances meet, — then silent ease
Spread o'er the multitude by slow degrees.

XLI.

Then swelled the organ: up through choir and nave
   The music trembled with an inward thrill
Of bliss at its own grandeur: wave on wave
   Its flood of mellow thunder rose, until
The hushed air shivered with the throb it gave,
   Then, poising for a moment, it stood still,
And sank and rose again, to burst in spray
That wandered into silence far away.

XLII.

Like to a mighty heart the music seemed,
    That yearns with melodies it cannot speak,
Until, in grand despair of what it dreamed,
    In the agony of effort it doth break,
Yet triumphs breaking; on it rushed and streamed
    And wantoned in its might, as when a lake,
Long pent among the mountains, bursts its walls
And in one crowding gush leaps forth and falls.

XLIII.

Deeper and deeper shudders shook the air,
    As the huge bass kept gathering heavily,
Like thunder when it rouses in its lair,
    And with its hoarse growl shakes the low-hung sky:
It grew up like a darkness everywhere,
    Filling the vast cathedral; — suddenly,
From the dense mass a boy's clear treble broke
Like lightning, and the full-toned choir awoke.

XLIV.

Through gorgeous windows shone the sun aslant,
    Brimming the church with gold and purple mist,
Meet atmosphere to bosom that rich chant,
    Where fifty voices in one strand did twist
Their varicolored tones, and left no want
    To the delighted soul, which sank abyssed
In the warm music-cloud, while, far below,
The organ heaved its surges to and fro.

XLV.

As if a lark should suddenly drop dead
  While the blue air yet trembled with its song,
So snapped at once that music's golden thread,
  Struck by a nameless fear that leapt along
From heart to heart, and like a shadow spread
  With instantaneous shiver through the throng,
So that some glanced behind, as half aware
A hideous shape of dread were standing there.

XLVI.

As, when a crowd of pale men gather round,
  Watching an eddy in the leaden deep,
From which they deem the body of one drowned
  Will be cast forth, from face to face doth creep
An eager dread that holds all tongues fast bound,
  Until the horror, with a ghastly leap,
Starts up, its dead blue arms stretched aimlessly,
Heaved with the swinging of the careless sea, —

XLVII.

So in the faces of all these there grew,
  As by one impulse, a dark, freezing awe,
Which, with a fearful fascination drew
  All eyes toward the altar; damp and raw
The air grew suddenly, and no man knew
  Whether perchance his silent neighbor saw
The dreadful thing, which all were sure would rise
To scare the strained lids wider from their eyes.

XLVIII.

The incense trembled as it upward sent
　　Its slow, uncertain thread of wandering blue,
As 't were the only living element
　　In all the church, so deep the stillness grew;
It seemed one might have heard it, as it went,
　　Gi⁻e out an audible rustle, curling through
The midnight silence of that awe-struck air,
More hushed than death, though so much life was there.

XLIX.

Nothing they saw, but a low voice was heard
　　Threading the ominous silence of that fear,
Gentle and terrorless as if a bird,
　　Wakened by some volcano's glare, should cheer
The murk air with his song; yet every word
　　In the cathedral's farthest arch seemed near,
As if it spoke to every one apart,
Like the clear voice of conscience in each heart.

L.

" O Rest, to weary hearts thou art most dear!
　　O Silence, after life's bewildering din,
Thou art most welcome, whether in the sear
　　Days of our age thou comest, or we win
Thy poppy-wreath in youth! then wherefore here
　　Linger I yet, once free to enter in
At that wished gate which gentle Death doth ope,
Into the boundless realm of Strength and Hope?

LI.

" The realm of Hope it seems, amid the lack
  Of Hope's entire fulfilment in the clay ;
Beyond our cloud-horizon the soul's track
  Seems clear and happy into endless day ;
But, when we enter on it, we look back,
  Earth grows the fairer as 't is far away,
The horizon moves before us as we go,
And where the soul is there is food for woe.

LII.

" The clay falls from us, but the spirit still
  Is all unchanged, save in its destined rise
To higher beauty, which upon its will
  Depends, as here : not instantly allwise
And good we grow, nor gifted with the skill
  Wrong to discern from right with undazed eyes :
Still round us, only wider, the stern ring
Of darkness gathers, never vanishing.

LIII.

" Think not in death my love could ever cease ;
  If thou wast false, more need there is for me
Still to be true ; that slumber were not peace,
  If 't were unvisited with dreams of thee :
And thou hadst never heard such words as these,
  Save that in heaven I must ever be
Most comfortless and wretched, seeing this
Our unbaptized babe shut out from bliss.

LIV.

" This little spirit with imploring eyes
　Wanders alone the dreary wild of space ;
The shadow of his pain for ever lies
　Upon my soul in this new dwelling-place ;
His loneliness makes me in Paradise
　More lonely, and, unless I see his face,
Even here for grief could I lie down and die,
Save for my curse of immortality.

LV.

" World after world he sees around him swim
　Crowded with happy souls, that take no heed
Of the sad eyes that from the night's faint rim
　Gaze sick with longing on them as they speed
With golden gates, that only shut out him ;
　And shapes sometimes from Hell's abysses freed
Flap darkly by him, with enormous sweep
Of wings that roughen wide the pitchy deep.

LVI.

" I am a mother, — spirits do not shake
　This much of earth from them, — and I must pine
Till I can feel his little hands and take
　His weary head upon this heart of mine ;
And, might it be, full gladly for his sake
　Would I this solitude of bliss resign,
And be shut out of Heaven to dwell with him
Forever in that silence drear and dim.

LVII.

" I strove to hush my soul, and would not speak
  At first, for thy dear sake ; a woman's love
Is mighty, but a mother's heart is weak,
  And by its weakness overcomes ; I strove
To smother bitter thoughts with patience meek,
  But still in the abyss my soul would rove,
Seeking my child, and drove me here to claim
The rite that gives him peace in Christ's dear name.

LVIII.

" I sit and weep while blessed spirits sing ;
  I can but long and pine the while they praise,
And, leaning o'er the wall of Heaven, I fling
  My voice to where I deem my infant strays,
Like a robbed bird that cries in vain to bring
  Her nestlings back beneath her wings' embrace ;
But still he answers not, and I but know
That Heaven and earth are both alike in woe.

LIX.

" And thou, dear Mordred, after penance done,
  By blessed Mary's grace may'st meet me here,
For she it was that pitied my sad moan,
  Herself not free from mother's pangs whilere,
And gave me leave to wander forth alone
  To ask due rites for him I held so dear :
When Holy Church shall grant his soul release,
I shall possess my heart and be at peace.

LX.

" Yes, ages hence, in joy we yet may meet,
    By sorrow thou, and I by patience, tried ;
No steep is hard for love's white feet to climb,
    And faith is but ambition purified,
And hope and memory would still be sweet,
    Though every other joy were quite denied ;
So let us look toward our gleam of light,
Although between lie leagues of barren night."

LXI.

Then the pale priests, with ceremony due,
    Baptized the child within its dreadful tomb
Beneath that mother's heart, whose instinct true
    Star-like had battled down the triple gloom
Of sorrow, love, and death : young maidens, too,
    Strewed the pale corpse with many a milkwhite
        bloom,
And parted the bright hair, and on the breast
Crossed the unconscious hands in sign of rest.

LXII.

Some said, that, when the priest had sprinkled o'er
    The consecrated drops, they seemed to hear
A sigh, as of some heart from travail sore
    Released, and then two voices singing clear,
Misereatur Deus, more and more
    Fading far upward, and their ghastly fear
Fell from them with that sound, as bodies fall
From souls upspringing to celestial hall.

LXIII.

And Mordred seemed to hear it and to grow
  Lighter at heart, and they who marked him said,
That something of the darkness of his woe
  Had from his stony eyes and visage fled,
Which glimmered now with a strange inward glow,
  As when the sun, with tempest-rack o'erspread,
Bursts through a sidelong rift, and on his scalp
Goldens afar some huge cloud-built Alp.

LXIV.

But when they sought him he was stark and cold,
  The loathing spirit had spurned off the clay
That to such crime had made it overbold:
  Upon his breast a little blossom lay
Of amaranth, such as grows not in earth's mould;
  Whence it had come or how could no man say,
But, after years had passed, it only showed
The fresher, and its gold more deeply glowed.

ALLEGRA.

I would more natures were like thine,
  That never casts a glance before, —
Thou Hebe, who thy heart's bright wine
  So lavishly to all dost pour,
That we who drink forget to pine,
  And can but dream of bliss in store.

Thou canst not see a shade in life;
  With sunward instinct thou dost rise,
And, leaving clouds below at strife,
  Gazest undazzled at the skies,
With all their blazing splendors rife,
  A songful lark with eagle's eyes.

Thou wast some foundling whom the Hours
  Nursed, laughing, with the milk of Mirth;
Some influence more gay than ours
  Hath ruled thy nature from its birth,
As if thy natal-stars were flowers
  That shook their seeds round thee on earth.

And thou, to lull thine infant rest,
  Wast cradled like an Indian child;
All pleasant winds from south and west
  With lullabies thine ears beguiled,
Rocking thee in thine oriole's nest,
  Till Nature looked at thee and smiled.

Thine every fancy seems to borrow
  A sunlight from thy childish years,
Making a golden cloud of sorrow,
  A hope-lit rainbow out of tears, —
Thy heart is certain of to-morrow,
  Though 'yond to-day it never peers.

I would more natures were like thine,
  So innocently wild and free,
Whose sad thoughts, even, leap and shine,
  Like sunny wavelets in the sea,
Making us mindless of the brine
  In gazing on the brilliancy.

THE FOUNTAIN.

INTO the sunshine,
  Full of the light,
Leaping and flashing
  From morn till night!

Into the moonlight,
  Whiter than snow,
Waving so flower-like
  When the winds blow!

Into the starlight
  Rushing in spray,
Happy at midnight,
  Happy by day!

Ever in motion,
  Blithesome and cheery,
Still climbing heavenward,
  Never aweary; —

Glad of all weathers,
  Still seeming best,
Upward or downward,
  Motion thy rest ; —

Full of a nature
  Nothing can tame,
Changed every moment,
  Ever the same ; —

Ceaseless aspiring,
  Ceaseless content,
Darkness or sunshine
  Thy element ; —

Glorious fountain !
  Let my heart be
Fresh, changeful, constant,
  Upward, like thee !

THE SHEPHERD OF KING ADMETUS.

THERE came a youth upon the earth,
  Some thousand years ago,
Whose slender hands were nothing worth,
Whether to plough, or reap, or sow.

He made a lyre, and drew therefrom
  Music so strange and rich,
That all men loved to hear, — and some
Muttered of fagots for a witch.

But King Admetus, one who had
   Pure taste by right divine,
Decreed his singing not too bad
To hear between the cups of wine :

And so, well-pleased with being soothed
   Into a sweet half-sleep,
Three times his kingly beard he smoothed
And made him viceroy o'er his sheep.

His words were simple words enough
   And yet he used them so,
That what in other mouths were rough
In his seemed musical and low.

Men called him but a shiftless youth,
   In whom no good they saw ;
And yet, unwittingly, in truth,
They made his careless words their law.

They knew not how he learned at all,
   For, long hour after hour,
He sat and watched the dead leaves fall,
Or mused upon a common flower.

It seemed the loveliness of things
   Did teach him all their use,
For, in mere weeds, and stones, and springs,
He found a healing power profuse.

Men granted that his speech was wise,
  But, when a glance they caught
Of his slim grace and woman's eyes,
They laughed, and called him good-for-naught.

Yet after he was dead and gone,
  And e'en his memory dim,
Earth seemed more sweet to live upon,
More full of love, because of him.

And day by day more holy grew
  Each spot where he had trod,
Till after-poets only knew
Their firstborn brother as a god.
  1842.

———

THE TOKEN.

It is a mere wild rosebud,
  Quite sallow now, and dry,
Yet there 's something wondrous in it, —
  Some gleams of days gone by, —
Dear sights and sounds that are to me
The fingerposts of memory,
And stir my heart's blood far below
Its short-lived waves of joy and woe.

Lips must fade and roses wither,
  All sweet times be o'er, —
They only smile, and, murmuring " Thither ! "
  Stay with us no more :

And yet oft-times a look or smile,
Forgotten in a kiss's while,
Years after from the dark will start,
And flash across the trembling heart.

Thou hast given me many roses,
  But never one, like this,
O'erfloods both sense and spirit
  With such a deep, wild bliss; —
We must have instincts that glean up
Sparse drops of this life in the cup,
Whose taste shall give us all that we
Can prove of immortality.

Earth's stablest things are shadows,
  And, in the life to come,
Haply some chance-saved trifle
  May tell of this old home:
As now sometimes we seem to find,
In a dark crevice of the mind,
Some relic, which, long pondered o'er,
Hints faintly at a life before.

———

SONG.

THERE is a light in thy blue eyes,
  Like an eternal morn,
A glorious freshness of the skies,
  That dulls not, nor is worn,
Though all earth's flitting shadows try
Its sunny immortality.

From thee I learn all gentleness,
From thee I learn all truth ;
And, from thy brimming heart's excess,
My spirit garners youth,
Gleaning, in harvest-hours like this,
Ripe winter-stores of golden bliss.

O, happy soul ! O, happy heart !
O, happy dreams of mine !
That thus can linger all apart
Within so charmed a shrine,
While the old weary earth turns round
With all its strife of empty sound !

1841.

LOVE.

TRUE Love is but a humble, low-born thing,
And hath its food served up in earthen ware ;
It is a thing to walk with, hand in hand,
Through the every-dayness of this work-day world,
Baring its tender feet to every roughness,
Yet letting not one heart-beat go astray
From Beauty's law of plainness and content ;
A simple, fire-side thing, whose quiet smile
Can warm earth's poorest hovel to a home ;
Which, when our autumn cometh, as it must,
And life in the chill wind shivers bare and leafless,
Shall still be blest with Indian-summer youth
In bleak November, and, with thankful heart,

Smile on its ample stores of garnered fruit,
As full of sunshine to our aged eyes
As when it nursed the blossoms of our spring.
Such is true Love, which steals into the heart
With feet as silent as the lightsome dawn
That kisses smooth the rough brows of the dark,
And hath its will through blissful gentleness, —
Not like a rocket, which, with savage glare,
Whirrs suddenly up, then bursts, and leaves the
        night
Painfully quivering on the dazed eyes;
A love that gives and takes, that seeth faults,
Not with flaw-seeking eyes like needle-points,
But, loving kindly, ever looks them down
With the o'ercoming faith of meek forgiveness;
A love that shall be new and fresh each hour,
As is the golden mystery of sunset,
Or the sweet coming of the evening-star,
Alike, and yet most unlike, every day,
And seeming ever best and fairest *now;*
A love that doth not kneel for what it seeks,
But faces Truth and Beauty as their peer,
Showing its worthiness of noble thoughts
By a clear sense of inward nobleness;
A love that in its object findeth not
All grace and beauty, and enough to sate
Its thirst of blessing, but, in all of good
Found there, it sees but Heaven-granted types
Of good and beauty in the soul of man,
And traces, in the simplest heart that beats,
A family-likeness to its chosen one,

That claims of it the rights of brotherhood.
For Love is blind but with the fleshly eye,
That so its inner sight may be more clear;
And outward shows of beauty only so
Are needful at the first, as is a hand
To guide and to uphold an infant's steps:
Great spirits need them not; their earnest look
Pierces the body's mask of thin disguise,
And beauty ever is to them revealed,
Behind the unshapeliest, meanest lump of clay,
With arms outstretched and eager face ablaze,
Yearning to be but understood and loved.

1840.

TO PERDITA, SINGING.

Thy voice is like a fountain,
    Leaping up in clear moonshine;
Silver, silver, ever mounting,
        Ever sinking,
        Without thinking,
    To that brimful heart of thine.

Every sad and happy feeling,
    Thou hast had in bygone years,
Through thy lips come stealing, stealing,
        Clear and low;
    All thy smiles and all thy tears
        In thy voice awaken,
And sweetness, wove of joy and woe,
    From their teaching it hath taken:

Feeling and music move together,
Like a swan and shadow, ever
Heaving on a sky-blue river
In a day of cloudless weather.

It hath caught a touch of sadness,
   Yet it is not sad ;
It hath tones of clearest gladness,
   Yet it is not glad ;
A dim, sweet, twilight voice it is,
   Where to-day's accustomed blue
Is over-grayed with memories,
   With starry feelings quivered through.

Thy voice is like a fountain
Leaping up in sunshine bright,
   And I never weary counting
Its clear droppings, lone and single,
Or when in one full gush they mingle,
   Shooting in melodious light.

Thine is music such as yields
Feelings of old brooks and fields,
And, around this pent-up room,
Sheds a woodland, free perfume ;
   O, thus for ever sing to me !
     O, thus for ever !
The green, bright grass of childhood bring to me,
   Flowing like an emerald river,
   And the bright-blue skies above !
   O, sing them back, as fresh as ever,

Into the bosom of my love, —
The sunshine and the merriment,
The unsought, evergreen content,
   Of that never cold time,
The joy, that, like a clear breeze, went
    Through and through the old time !

Peace sits within thine eyes,
With white hands crossed in joyful rest,
While, through thy lips and face, arise
The melodies from out thy breast ;
      She sits and sings,
      With folded wings
      And white arms crost,
  " Weep not for passed things,
      They are not lost :
The beauty which the summer time
O'er thine opening spirit shed,
The forest oracles sublime
That filled thy soul with joyous dread,
The scent of every smallest flower
That made thy heart sweet for an hour, —
Yea, every holy influence,
Flowing to thee, thou knewest not whence,
In thine eyes to-day is seen,
Fresh as it hath ever been ;
Promptings of Nature, beckonings sweet,
Whatever led thy childish feet,
Still will linger unawares
The guiders of thy silver hairs ;
Every look and every word

Which thou givest forth to-day,
Tell of the singing of the bird
Whose music stilled thy boyish play."
Thy voice is like a fountain,
Twinkling up in sharp starlight,
When the moon behind the mountain
Dims the low East with faintest white,
  Ever darkling,
  Ever sparkling,
We know not if 't is dark or bright;
But, when the great moon hath rolled round,
And, sudden-slow, its solemn power
Grows from behind its black, clear-edged bound,
No spot of dark the fountain keepeth,
But, swift as opening eyelids, leapeth
Into a waving silver flower.

1841

THE FORLORN.

THE night is dark, the stinging sleet,
 Swept by the bitter gusts of air,
Drives whistling down the lonely street,
 And stiffens on the pavement bare.

The street-lamps flare and struggle dim
 Through the white sleet-clouds as they pass,
Or, governed by a boisterous whim,
 Drop down and rattle on the glass.

One poor, heart-broken, outcast girl
    Faces the east-wind's searching flaws,
And, as about her heart they whirl,
    Her tattered cloak more tightly draws.

The flat brick walls look cold and bleak,
    Her bare feet to the sidewalk freeze;
Yet dares she not a shelter seek,
    Though faint with hunger and disease.

The sharp storm cuts her forehead bare,
    And, piercing through her garments thin,
Beats on her shrunken breast, and there
    Makes colder the cold heart within.

She lingers where a ruddy glow
    Streams outward through an open shutter,
Giving more bitterness to woe,
    More loneness to desertion utter.

One half the cold she had not felt,
    Until she saw this gush of light
Spread warmly forth, and seem to melt
    Its slow way through the deadening night.

She hears a woman's voice within,
    Singing sweet words her childhood knew,
And years of misery and sin
    Furl off and leave her heaven blue.

Her freezing heart, like one who sinks
   Outwearied in the drifting snow,
Drowses to deadly sleep, and thinks
   No longer of its hopeless woe:

Old fields, and clear blue summer days,
   Old meadows, green with grass and trees,
That shimmer through the trembling haze
   And whiten in the western breeze, —

Old faces, — all the friendly past
   Rises within her heart again,
And sunshine from her childhood cast
   Makes summer of the icy rain.

Enhaloed by a mild, warm glow,
   From all humanity apart,
She hears old footsteps wandering slow
   Through the lone chambers of her heart.

Outside the porch before the door,
   Her cheek upon the cold, hard stone
She lies, no longer foul and poor,
   No longer dreary and alone.

Next morning, something heavily
   Against the opening door did weigh,
And there, from sin and sorrow free,
   A woman on the threshold lay.

A smile upon the wan lips told
    That she had found a calm release,
And that, from out the want and cold,
    The song had borne her soul in peace.

For, whom the heart of Man shuts out,
    Straightway the heart of God takes in,
And fences them all round about
    With silence mid the world's loud din;

And one of his great charities
    Is Music, and it doth not scorn
To close the lids upon the eyes
    Of the polluted and forlorn;

Far was she from her childhood's home,
    Farther in guilt had wandered thence,
Yet thither it had bid her come
    To die in maiden innocence.
    1842.

SONG.

O MOONLIGHT deep and tender,
    A year and more agone,
Your mist of golden splendor
    Round my betrothal shone!

O elm-leaves dark and dewy,
    The very same ye seem,
The low wind trembles through ye,
    Ye murmur in my dream!

O river, dim with distance,
 Flow thus forever by,
A part of my existence
 Within your heart doth lie!

O stars, ye saw our meeting,
 Two beings and one soul,
Two hearts so madly beating
 To mingle and be whole!

 O happy night, deliver
 Her kisses back to me,
Or keep them all, and give her
 A blissful dream of me!
1842.

———

MIDNIGHT.

THE moon shines white and silent
 On the mist, which, like a tide
Of some enchanted ocean,
 O'er the wide marsh doth glide,
Spreading its ghost-like billows
 Silently far and wide.

A vague and starry magic
 Makes all things mysteries,
And lures the earth's dumb spirit
 Up to the longing skies, —
I seem to hear dim whispers,
 And tremulous replies.

The fireflies o'er the meadow
  In pulses come and go;
The elmtrees' heavy shadow
  Weighs on the grass below;
And faintly from the distance
  The dreaming cock doth crow.

All things look strange and mystic,
  The very bushes swell
And take wild shapes and motions,
  As if beneath a spell, —
They seem not the same lilacs
  From childhood known so well.

The snow of deepest silence
  O'er everything doth fall,
So beautiful and quiet,
  And yet so like a pall,
As if all life were ended,
  And rest were come to all.

O, wild and wondrous midnight,
  There is a might in thee
To make the charmed body
  Almost like spirit be,
And give it some faint glimpses
  Of immortality!

1842.

APPLEDORE.

How looks Appledore in a storm?
　　I have seen it when its crags seemed frantic,
　　Butting against the maddened Atlantic,
When surge after surge would heap enorme,
　　Cliffs of Emerald topped with snow,
　　That lifted and lifted and then let go
A great white avalanche of thunder,
　　A grinding, blinding, deafening ire
Monadnock might have trembled under;
　　And the island, whose rock-roots pierce below
　　To where they are warmed with the central fire,
You could feel its granite fibres racked,
　　As it seemed to plunge with a shudder and thrill
　　Right at the breast of the swooping hill,
And to rise again, snorting a cataract
Of rage-froth from every cranny and ledge,
　　While the sea drew its breath in hoarse and deep,
And the next vast breaker curled its edge,
　　Gathering itself for a mighty leap.
North, east, and south there are reefs and breakers,
　　You would never dream of in smooth weather,
That toss and gore the sea for acres,
　　Bellowing and gnashing and snarling together;
Look northward, where Duck Island lies,
And over its crown you will see arise,
Against a background of slaty skies,
　　A row of pillars still and white
　　That glimmer and then are out of sight,

As if the moon should suddenly kiss,
  While you crossed the gusty desert by night,
The long colonnades of Persepolis,
And then as sudden a darkness would follow
To gulp the whole scene at a single swallow,
The city's ghost, the drear, brown waste,
And the string of camels, clumsy-paced : —
Look southward for White Island light,
  The lantern stands ninety feet o'er the tide ;
There is first a half-mile of tumult and fight,
Of dash and roar and tumble and fright,
  And surging bewilderment wild and wide,
Where the breakers struggle left and right,
  Then a mile or more of rushing sea,
And then the light-house slim and lone ;
And whenever the whole weight of ocean is thrown
Full and fair on White Island head,
  A great mist-jotun you will see
  Lifting himself up silently
High and huge o'er the light-house top,
With hands of wavering spray outspread,
  Groping after the little tower,
  That seems to shrink, and shorten and cower,
Till the monster's arms of a sudden drop,
  And silently and fruitlessly
  He sinks again into the sea.

You, meanwhile, where drenched you stand,
  Awaken once more to the rush and roar
And on the rock-point tighten your hand,
As you turn and see a valley deep,

That was not there a moment before,
Sack rattling down between you and a heap
   Of toppling billow, whose instant fall
   Must sink the whole island once for all —
Or watch the silenter, stealthier seas
   Feeling their way to you more and more;
If they once should clutch you high as the knees
They would whirl you down like a sprig of kelp,
Beyond all reach of hope or help; —
   And such in a storm is Appledore.

TO THE DANDELION.

DEAR common flower, that grow'st beside the way,
Fringing the dusty road with harmless gold,
   First pledge of blithesome May,
Which children pluck, and, full of pride, uphold,
High-hearted buccaneers, o'erjoyed that they
An Eldorado in the grass have found,
   Which not the rich earth's ample round
May match in wealth — thou art more dear to me
Than all the prouder Summer-blooms may be.

Gold such as thine ne'er drew the Spanish prow
Through the primeval hush of Indian seas,
   Nor wrinkled the lean brow
Of age, to rob the lover's heart of ease;
'Tis the Spring's largess, which she scatters now
To rich and poor alike, with lavish hand,
   Though most hearts never understand
To take it at God's value, but pass by
The offered wealth with unrewarded eye.

Thou art my tropics and mine Italy;
To look at thee unlocks a warmer clime;
   The eyes thou givest me
Are in the heart and heed not space or time:
Not in mid June the golden-cuirassed bee
Feels a more Summer-like, warm ravishment
   In the white lily's breezy tent,
His fragrant Sybaris, than I, when first
From the dark green thy yellow circles burst.

Then think I of deep shadows in the grass, —
Of meadows where in sun the cattle graze,
   Where, as the breezes pass,
The gleaming rushes lean a thousand ways, —
Of leaves that slumber in a cloudy mass,
Or whiten in the wind, — of waters blue
   That from the distance sparkle through
Some woodland gap, — and of a sky above
Where one white cloud like a stray lamb doth move.

My childhood's earliest thoughts are linked with
     thee;
The sight of thee calls back the robin's song,
   Who from the dark old tree
Beside the door, sang clearly all day long,
And I, secure in childish piety,
Listened as if I heard an angel sing
   With news from Heaven, which he could bring
Fresh every day to my untainted ears,
When birds and flowers and I were happy peers.

Thou art the type of those meek charities
Which make up half the nobleness of life,
  Those cheap delights the wise
Pluck from the dusty wayside of earth's strife;
Words of frank cheer, glances of friendly eyes,
Love's smallest coin, which yet to some may give
  The morsel that may keep alive
A starving heart, and teach it to behold
Some glimpse of God where all before was cold.

Thy wingèd seeds, whereof the winds take care,
Are like the words of poet and of sage
  Which through the free heaven fare,
And, now unheeded, in another age
Take root, and to the gladdened future bear
That witness which the present would not heed,
  Bringing forth many a thought and deed,
And, planted safely in the eternal sky,
Bloom into stars which earth is guided by.

Full of deep love thou art, yet not more full
Than all thy common brethren of the ground,
  Wherein, were we not dull,
Some words of highest wisdom might be found;
Yet earnest faith from day to day may cull
Some syllables, which, rightly joined, can make
  A spell to soothe life's bitterest ache,
And ope Heaven's portals, which are near us still,
Yea, nearer ever than the gates of Ill.

How like a prodigal doth nature seem,
When thou, for all thy gold, so common art!
   Thou teachest me to deem
More sacredly of every human heart,
Since each reflects in joy its scanty gleam
Of Heaven, and could some wondrous secret show,
   Did we but pay the love we owe,
And with a child's undoubting wisdom look
On all these living pages of God's book.

But let me read thy lesson right or no,
Of one good gift from thee my heart is sure;
   Old I shall never grow
While thou each year dost come to keep me pure
With legends of my childhood; ah, we owe
Well more than half life's holiness to these
   Nature's first lowly influences,
At thought of which the heart's glad doors burst ope,
In dreariest days, to welcome peace and hope.

DARA.

WHEN Persia's sceptre trembled in a hand
Wilted by harem-heats, and all the land
   Was hovered over by those vulture ills
That snuff decaying empire from afar,
Then, with a nature balanced as a star,
   Dara arose, a shepherd of the hills.

He, who had governed fleecy subjects well,
Made his own village, by the self-same spell,
  Secure and peaceful as a guarded fold,
Till, gathering strength by slow and wise degrees,
Under his sway, to neighbor villages
  Order returned, and faith and justice old.

Now, when it fortuned that a king more wise
Endued the realm with brain and hands and eyes,
  He sought on every side men brave and just,
And having heard the mountain-shepherd's praise,
How he rendered the mould of elder days,
  To Dara gave a satrapy in trust.

So Dara shepherded a province wide,
Nor in his viceroy's sceptre took more pride
  Than in his crook before; but Envy finds
More soil in cities than on mountains bare,
And the frank sun of spirits clear and rare
  Breeds poisonous fogs in low and marish minds.

Soon it was whispered at the royal ear
That, though wise Dara's province, year by year,
  Like a great sponge, drew wealth and plenty up,
Yet, when he squeezed it at the king's behest,
Some golden drops, more rich than all the rest,
  Went to the filling of his private cup.

For proof, they said that wheresoe'er he went
A chest, beneath whose weight the camel bent,
  Went guarded, and no other eye had seen

What was therein, save only Dara's own,
Yet when 't was opened, all his tent was known
　　To glow and lighten with heapt jewels' sheen.

The king set forth for Dara's province straight,
Where, as was fit, outside his city's gate
　　The viceroy met him with a stately train ;
And there, with archers circled, close at hand,
A camel with the chest was seen to stand,
　　The king grew red, for thus the guilt was plain.

" Open me now," he cried, " yon treasure-chest ! "
'T was done, and only a worn shepherd's vest
　　Was found within ; some blushed and hung the head,
Not Dara ; open as the sky's blue roof
He stood, and " O, my lord, behold the proof
　　That I was worthy of my trust ! " he said.

" For ruling men, lo ! all the charm I had ;
My soul, in those coarse vestments ever clad,
　　Still to the unstained past kept true and leal,
Still on these plains could breathe her mountain air,
And Fortune's heaviest gifts serenely bear,
　　Which bend men from the truth, and make them
　　　　reel.

" To govern wisely I had shown small skill
Were I not lord of simple Dara still ;
　　That sceptre kept, I cannot lose my way ! "
Strange dew in royal eyes grew round and bright
And thrilled the trembling lids ; before 't was night
　　Two added provinces blessed Dara's sway.

TO J. F. H.

NINE years have slipped like hour-glass sand
    From life's fast-emptying globe away,
Since last, dear friend, I clasped your hand,
And lingered on the impoverished land,
    Watching the steamer down the bay.

I held the keepsake which you gave,
    Until the dim smoke-pennon curled
O'er the vague rim 'tween sky and wave,
And closed the distance like a grave,
    Leaving me to the outer world;

The old worn world of hurry and heat,
    The young, fresh world of thought and scope;
While you, where silent surges fleet
Toward far sky beaches still and sweet,
    Sunk wavering down the ocean-slope.

Come back our ancient walks to tread,
    Old haunts of lost or scattered friends,
Amid the Muses' factories red,
Where song, and smoke, and laughter sped
    The nights to proctor-hunted ends.

Our old familiars are not laid,
    Though snapped our wands and sunk our books,
    They beckon, not to be gainsaid,
Where, round broad meads which mowers wade,
    Smooth Charles his steel-blue sickle crooks;

Where, as the cloudbergs eastward blow,
  From glow to gloom the hillside shifts
Its lakes of rye that surge and flow,
Its plumps of orchard-trees arow,
  Its snowy white-weed's summer drifts.

Or let us to Nantasket, there
  To wander idly as we list,
Whether, on rocky hillocks bare,
Sharp cedar-points, like breakers, tear
  The trailing fringes of gray mist.

Or whether, under skies clear-blown,
  The heightening surfs with foamy din,
Their breeze-caught forelocks backward blown
Against old Neptune's yellow zone,
  Curl slow, and plunge forever in.

For years thrice three, wise Horace said,
  A poem rare let silence bind;
And love may ripen in the shade,
Like ours, for nine long seasons laid
  In crypts and arches of the mind.

That right Falernian friendship old
  Will we, to grace our feast, call up,
And freely pour the juice of gold,
That keeps life's pulses warm and bold,
  Till Death shall break the empty cup.

ROSALINE.

THOU look'd'st on me all yesternight,
Thine eyes were blue, thy hair was bright
As when we murmured our trothplight
Beneath the thick stars, Rosaline!
Thy hair was braided on thy head
As on the day we two were wed,
Mine eyes scarce knew if thou wert dead —
But my shrunk heart knew, Rosaline!

The deathwatch tickt behind the wall,
The blackness rustled like a pall,
The moaning wind did rise and fall
Among the bleak pines, Rosaline!
My heart beat thickly in mine ears:
The lids may shut out fleshly fears,
But still the spirit sees and hears,
Its eyes are lidless, Rosaline!

A wildness rushing suddenly,
A knowing some ill shape is nigh,
A wish for death, a fear to die —
Is not this vengeance, Rosaline!
A loneliness that is not lone,
A love quite withered up and gone,
A strong soul trampled from its throne —
What would'st thou further, Rosaline!

'T is lone such moonless nights as these,
Strange sounds are out upon the breeze,
And the leaves shiver in the trees,
And then thou comest, Rosaline!
I seem to hear the mourners go,
With long black garments trailing slow,
And plumes a-nodding to and fro,
As once I heard them, Rosaline!

Thy shroud it is of snowy white,
And, in the middle of the night,
Thou standest moveless and upright,
Gazing upon me, Rosaline!
There is no sorrow in thine eyes,
But evermore that meek surprise —
Oh, God! her gentle spirit tries
To deem me guiltless, Rosaline!

Above thy grave the robin sings,
And swarms of bright and happy things
Flit all about with sunlit wings —
But I am cheerless. Rosaline!
The violets on the hillock toss,
The gravestone is o'ergrown with moss,
For nature feels not any loss —
But I am cheerless, Rosaline!

Ah! why wert thou so lowly bred?
Why was my pride galled on to wed
Her who brought lands and gold instead
Of thy heart's treasure, Rosaline!

" Oh, God! her gentle spirit tries
To deem me guiltless, Rosaline!"

Why did I fear to let thee stay
To look on me and pass away
Forgivingly, as in its May,
A broken flower, Rosaline!

I thought not, when my dagger strook,
Of thy blue eyes; I could not brook
The past all pleading in one look
Of utter sorrow, Rosaline!
I did not know when thou wert dead:
A blackbird whistling overhead
Thrilled through my brain; I would have fled
But dared not leave thee, Rosaline!

A low, low moan, a light twig stirred
By the upspringing of a bird,
A drip of blood — were all I heard —
Then deathly stillness, Rosaline!
The sun rolled down, and very soon,
Like a great fire, the awful moon
Rose, stained with blood, and then a swoon
Crept chilly o'er me, Rosaline!

The stars came out; and, one by one,
Each angel from his silver throne
Looked down and saw what I had done:
I dared not hide me, Rosaline!
I crouched; I feared thy corpse would cry
Against me to God's quiet sky,
I thought I saw the blue lips try
To utter something, Rosaline!

I waited with a maddened grin
To hear that voice all icy thin
Slide forth and tell my deadly sin
To hell and heaven, Rosaline!
But no voice came, and then it seemed
That if the very corpse had screamed
The sound like sunshine glad had streamed
Through that dark stillness, Rosaline!

Dreams of old quiet glimmered by,
And faces loved in infancy
Came and looked on me mournfully,
Till my heart melted, Rosaline!
I saw my mother's dying bed,
I heard her bless me, and I shed
Cool tears — but lo! the ghastly dead
Stared me to madness, Rosaline!

And then amid the silent night
I screamed with horrible delight,
And in my brain an awful light
Did seem to crackle, Rosaline!
It is my curse! sweet mem'ries fall
From me like snow — and only all
Of that one night, like cold worms crawl
My doomed heart over, Rosaline!

Thine eyes are shut: they nevermore
Will leap thy gentle words before
To tell the secret o'er and o'er
Thou could'st not smother, Rosaline!

Thine eyes are shut: they will not shine
With happy tears, or, through the vine
That hid thy casement, beam on mine
Sunfull with gladness, Rosaline!

Thy voice I nevermore shall hear,
Which in old times did seem so dear,
That, ere it trembled in mine ear,
My quick heart heard it, Rosaline!
Would I might die! I were as well,
Ay, better, at my home in hell,
To set for aye a burning spell
'Twixt me and memory, Rosaline!

Why wilt thou haunt me with thine eyes,
Wherein such blessed memories,
Such pitying forgiveness lies,
Than hate more bitter, Rosaline!
Woe 's me! I know that love so high
As thine, true soul, could never die,
And with mean clay in churchyard lie —
Would God it were so, Rosaline!

———

SONNET.

IF some small savor creep into my rhyme
Of the old poets, if some words I use,
Neglected long, which have the lusty thews
Of that gold-haired and earnest-hearted time,
Whose loving joy and sorrow all sublime

Have given our tongue its starry eminence, —
It is not pride, God knows, but reverence
Which hath grown in me since my childhood's
    prime ;
Wherein I feel that my poor lyre is strung
With soul-strings like to theirs, and that I have
No right to muse their holy graves among,
If I can be a custom-fettered slave,
And, in mine own true spirit, am not brave
To speak what rusheth upward to my tongue.

A GLANCE BEHIND THE CURTAIN.

WE see but half the causes of our deeds,
Seeking them wholly in the outer life,
And heedless of the encircling spirit-world
Which, though unseen, is felt, and sows in us
All germs of pure and world-wide purposes.
From one stage of our being to the next
We pass unconscious o'er a slender bridge,
The momentary work of unseen hands,
Which crumbles down behind us ; looking back,
We see the other shore, the gulf between,
And, marvelling how we won to where we stand,
Content ourselves to call the builder Chance.
We trace the wisdom to the apple's fall,
Not to the soul of Newton, ripe with all
The hoarded thoughtfulness of earnest years,
And waiting but one ray of sunlight more
To blossom fully.

But whence came that ray?
We call our sorrows destiny, but ought
Rather to name our high successes so.
Only the instincts of great souls are Fate,
And have predestined sway: all other things,
Except by leave of us, could never be.
For Destiny is but the breath of God
Still moving in us, the last fragment left
Of our unfallen nature, waking oft
Within our thought to beckon us beyond
The narrow circle of the seen and known,
And always tending to a noble end,
As all things must that overrule the soul,
And for a space unseat the helmsman, Will.
The fate of England and of freedom once
Seemed wavering in the heart of one plain man;
One step of his, and the great dial-hand
That marks the destined progress of the world
In the eternal round from wisdom on
To higher wisdom, had been made to pause
A hundred years. That step he did not take —
He knew not why, nor we, but only God —
And lived to make his simple oaken chair
More terrible and grandly beautiful,
More full of majesty, than any throne,
Before or after, of a British king.

Upon the pier stood two stern-visaged men,
Looking to where a little craft lay moored,
Swayed by the lazy current of the Thames,
Which weltered by in muddy listlessness.

Grave men they were, and battlings of fierce thought
Had scared away all softness from their brows,
And ploughed rough furrows there before their time.
Care, not of self, but of the common weal,
Had robbed their eyes of youth, and left instead
A look of patient power and iron will,
And something fiercer, too, that gave broad hint
Of the plain weapons girded at their sides.
The younger had an aspect of command —
Not such as trickles down, a slender stream,
In the shrunk channel of a great descent —
But such as lies entowered in heart and head,
And an arm prompt to do the 'hests of both.
His was a brow where gold were out of place,
And yet it seemed right worthy of a crown
(Though he despisèd such), were it only made
Of iron, or some serviceable stuff
That would have matched his sinewy brown face.
The elder, although such he hardly seemed
(Care makes so little of some five short years),
Bore a clear, honest face, where scholarship
Had mildened somewhat of its rougher strength,
To sober courage, such as best befits
The unsullied temper of a well-taught mind,
Yet left it so as one could plainly guess
The pent volcano smouldering underneath.
He spoke: the other, hearing, kept his gaze
Still fixed, as on some problem in the sky.

" O CROMWELL, we are fallen on evil times !
There was a day when England had wide room

For honest men as well as foolish kings;
But now the uneasy stomach of the time
Turns squeamish at them both.   Therefore let us
Seek out that savage clime where men as yet
Are free: there sleeps the vessel on the tide,
Her languid sails but drooping for the wind.
All things are fitly cared for, and the Lord
Will watch as kindly o'er the Exodus
Of us his servants now, as in old time.
We have no cloud or fire, and haply we
May not pass dryshod through the ocean-stream;
But, saved or lost, all things are in His hand."
So spake he, and meantime the other stood
With wide, gray eyes still reading the blank air,
As if upon the sky's blue wall he saw
Some mystic sentence written by a hand
Such as of old did scare the Assyrian king,
Girt with his satraps in the blazing feast.

"HAMPDEN, a moment since, my purpose was
To fly with thee — for I will call it flight,
Nor flatter it with any smoother name —
But something in me bids me not to go;
And I am one, thou knowest, who, unscared
By what the weak deem omens, yet give heed
And reverence due to whatsoe'er my soul
Whispers of warning to the inner ear.
Why should we fly?   Nay, why not rather stay
And rear again our Zion's crumbled walls,
Not as of old the walls of Thebes were built
By minstrel twanging, but, if need should be,

With the more potent music of our swords?
Think'st thou that score of men beyond the sea
Claim more God's care than all of England here?
No: when He moves His arm, it is to aid
Whole peoples, heedless if a few be crushed,
As some are ever when the destiny
Of man takes one stride onward nearer home.
Believe it, 't is the mass of men He loves,
And where there is most sorrow and most want,
Where the high heart of man is trodden down
The most, 't is not because He hides His face
From them in wrath, as purblind teachers prate.
Not so: there most is He, for there is He
Most needed.   Men who seek for Fate abroad
Are not so near His heart as they who dare
Frankly to face her where she faces them,
On their own threshold, where their souls are strong
To grapple with and throw her, as I once,
Being yet a boy, did throw this puny king,
Who now has grown so dotard as to deem
That he can wrestle with an angry realm,
And throw the brawned Antæus of men's rights.
No, Hampden; they have half-way conquered Fate
Who go half-way to meet her — as will I.
Freedom hath yet a work for me to do;
So speaks that inward voice which never yet
Spake falsely, when it urged the spirit on
To noble deeds for country and mankind.

" What should we do in that small colony
Of pinched fanatics, who would rather choose

Freedom to clip an inch more from their hair
Than the great chance of setting England free ?
Not there amid the stormy wilderness
Should we learn wisdom ; or, if learned, what room
To put it into act — else worse than naught ?
We learn our souls more, tossing for an hour
Upon this huge and ever vexèd sea
Of human thought, where kingdoms go to wreck
Like fragile bubbles yonder in the stream,
Than in a cycle of New England sloth,
Broke only by some petty Indian war,
Or quarrel for a letter, more or less,
In some hard word, which, spelt in either way,
Not their most learnèd clerks can understand.
New times demand new measures and new men ;
The world advances, and in time outgrows
The laws that in our father's day were best ;
And, doubtless, after us, some purer scheme
Will be shaped out by wiser men than we,
Made wiser by the steady growth of truth.
We cannot bring Utopia at once ;
But better almost be at work in sin
Than in a brute inaction browse and sleep.
No man is born into the world whose work
Is not born with him ; there is always work,
And tools to work withal, for those who will ;
And blessed are the horny hands of toil !
The busy world shoves angrily aside
The man who stands with arms a-kimbo set,
Until occasion tells him what to do ;
And he who waits to have his task marked out,

Shall die and leave his errand unfulfilled.
Our time is one that calls for earnest deeds.
Reason and Government, like two broad seas,
Yearn for each other with outstretched arms
Across this narrow isthmus of the throne.
And roll their white surf higher every day.
The field lies wide before us, where to reap
The easy harvest of a deathless name,
Though with no better sickles than our swords.
My soul is not a palace of the past,
Where outworn creeds, like Rome's gray senate
        quake,
Hearing afar the Vandal's trumpet hoarse,
That shakes old systems with a thunder-fit.
The time is ripe, and rotten-ripe, for change;
Then let it come: I have no dread of what
Is called for by the instinct of mankind.
Nor think I that God's world would fall apart
Because we tear a parchment more or less.
Truth is eternal, but her effluence,
With endless change, is fitted to the hour;
Her mirror is turned forward, to reflect
The promise of the future, not the past.
I do not fear to follow out the truth,
Albeit along the precipice's edge.
Let us speak plain: there is more force in names
Than most men dream of; and a lie may keep
Its throne a whole age longer, if it skulk
Behind the shield of some fair-seeming name.
Let us call tyrants *tyrants*, and maintain
That only freedom comes by grace of God.

And all that comes not by his grace must fall;
For men in earnest have no time to waste
In patching fig-leaves for the naked truth.

" I will have one more grapple with the man
Charles Stuart: whom the boy o'ercame,
The man stands not in awe of.   I perchance
Am one raised up by the Almighty arm
To witness some great truth to all the world.
Souls destined to o'erleap the vulgar lot,
And mould the world unto the scheme of God,
Have a foreconsciousness of their high doom,
As men are known to shiver at the heart,
When the cold shadow of some coming ill
Creeps slowly o'er their spirits unawares:
Hath Good less power of prophecy than Ill?
How else could men whom God hath called to sway
Earth's rudder, and to steer the barque of Truth
Beating against the wind toward her port,
Bear all the mean and buzzing grievances,
The petty martyrdoms wherewith Sin strives
To weary out the tethered hope of Faith,
The sneers, the unrecognizing look of friends,
Who worship the dead corpse of old king Custom,
Where it doth lie in state within the Church,
Striving to cover up the mighty ocean
With a man's palm, and making even the truth
Lie for them, holding up the glass reversed,
To make the hope of man seem further off?
My God! when I read o'er the bitter lives
Of men whose eager hearts were quite too great

To beat beneath the cramped mode of the day,
And see them mocked at by the world they love,
Haggling with prejudice for pennyworths
Of that reform which their hard toil will make
The common birthright of the age to come —
When I see this, spite of my faith in God,
I marvel how their hearts bear up so long;
Nor could they, but for this same prophecy,
This inward feeling of the glorious end.

" Deem me not fond; but in my warmer youth,
Ere my heart's bloom was soiled and brushed away,
I had great dreams of mighty things to come;
Of conquest; whether by the sword or pen,
I knew not; but some conquest I would have,
Or else swift death: now, wiser grown in years,
I find youth's dreams are but the flutterings
Of those strong wings whereon the soul shall soar
In after time to win a starry throne;
And therefore cherish them, for they were lots
Which I, a boy, cast in the helm of Fate.
Nor will I draw them, since a man's right hand,
A right hand guided by an earnest soul,
With a true instinct, takes the golden prize
From out a thousand blanks.   What men call luck,
Is the prerogative of valiant souls,
The fealty life pays its rightful kings.
The helm is shaking now, and I will stay
To pluck my lot forth; it were sin to flee ! "

So they two turned together; one to die
Fighting for freedom on the bloody field;
The other, far more happy, to become
A name earth wears forever next her heart;
One of the few that have a right to rank
With the true Makers; for his spirit wrought
Order from Chaos; proved that right divine
Dwelt only in the excellence of Truth;
And far within old Darkness' hostile lines
Advanced and pitched the shining tents of Light.
Nor shall the grateful Muse forget to tell,
That — not the least among his many claims
To deathless honor — he was MILTON's friend,
A man not second among those who lived
To show us that the poet's lyre demands
An arm of tougher sinew than the sword.

————

A SONG.

VIOLET! sweet violet!
  Thine eyes are full of tears;
      Are they wet
      Even yet
With the thought of other years,
Or with gladness are they full,
For the night so beautiful,
And longing for those far-off spheres?

Loved one of my youth thou wast,
Of my merry youth,
     And I see,
     Tearfully,
All the fair and sunny past,
All its openness and truth,
Ever fresh and green in thee
As the moss is in the sea.

Thy little heart, that hath with love
Grown colored like the sky above,
On which thou lookest ever, —
     Can it know
     All the woe
Of hope for what returneth never,
All the sorrow and the longing
To these hearts of ours belonging!

Out on it! no foolish pining
     For the sky
     Dims thine eye,
Or for the stars so calmly shining;
Like thee let this soul of mine
Take hue from that wherefor I long,
Self-stayed and high, serene and strong,
Not satisfied with hoping — but divine.

Violet! dear Violet!
Thy blue eyes are only wet
With joy and love of him who sent thee,
And for the fulfilling sense
Of that glad obedience
Which made thee all which Nature meant thee!

THE MOON.

My soul was like the sea
  Before the moon was made;
Moaning in vague immensity,
  Of its own strength afraid,
  Unrestful and unstaid.

Through every rift it foamed in vain
  About its earthly prison,
Seeking some unknown thing in pain,
And sinking restless back again,
  For yet no moon had risen:
Its only voice a vast dumb moan
Of utterless anguish speaking,
It lay unhopefully alone
And lived but in an aimless seeking.

So was my soul: but when 't was full
  Of unrest to o'erloading,
A voice of something beautiful
  Whispered a dim foreboding,
And yet so soft, so sweet, so low,
It had not more of joy than woe:
And, as the sea doth oft lie still,
  Making his waters meet,
As if by an unconscious will,
  For the moon's silver feet,
Like some serene, unwinking eye
That waits a certain destiny,
So lay my soul within mine eyes
When thou its sovereign moon didst rise.

And now, howe'er its waves above
  May toss and seem uneaseful,
One strong, eternal law of love
  With guidance sure and peaceful,
As calm and natural as breath
Moves its great deeps through Life and Death.

––––––––––

THE FATHERLAND.

WHERE is the true man's fatherland?
  Is it where he by chance is born?
  Doth not the free-winged spirit scorn
In such pent borders to be spanned?
  Oh yes! his fatherland must be
  As the blue heavens wide and free '

Is it alone where freedom is,
  Where God is God and man is man?
  Doth he not claim a broader span
For the soul's love of home than this?
  Oh yes! his fatherland must be
  As the blue heavens wide and free!

Where'er a human heart doth wear
  Joy's myrtle wreath, or sorrow's gyves,
  Where'er a human spirit strives
After a life more pure and fair,
  There is the true man's birthplace grand!
  His is a world-wide fatherland!

Where'er a single slave doth pine,
　Where'er one man may help another —
　Thank God for such a birthright, brother!
That spot of earth is thine and mine;
　There is the true man's birthplace grand!
　His is a world-wide fatherland!

———

A PARABLE.

WORN and footsore was the Prophet
　When he reached the holy hill;
" God has left the earth," he murmured,
　" Here his presence lingers still.

" God of all the olden prophets,
　Wilt thou talk with me no more?
Have I not as truly loved thee
　As thy chosen ones of yore?

" Hear me, guider of my fathers,
　Lo, an humble heart is mine;
By thy mercy I beseech thee,
　Grant thy servant but a sign!"

Bowing then his head, he listened
　For an answer to his prayer;
No loud burst of thunder followed,
　Not a murmur stirred the air:

But the tuft of moss before him
  Opened while he waited yet,
And from out the rock's hard bosom
  Sprang a tender violet.

" God ! I thank thee," said the Prophet,
  " Hard of heart and blind was I,
Looking to the holy mountain
  For the gift of prophecy.

" Still thou speakest with thy children
  Freely as in Eld sublime,
Humbleness and love and patience
  Give dominion over Time.

" Had I trusted in my nature,
  And had faith in lowly things,
Thou thyself wouldst then have sought me,
  And set free my spirit's wings.

" But I looked for signs and wonders
  That o'er men should give me sway;
Thirsting to be more than mortal,
  I was even less than clay.

" Ere I entered on my journey,
  As I girt my loins to start,
Ran to me my little daughter,
  The belovèd of my heart;

" In her hand she held a flower,
   Like to this as like may be,
Which beside my very threshold
   She had plucked and brought to me."

———————

ON THE DEATH OF A FRIEND'S CHILD.

DEATH never came so nigh to me before,
Nor showed me his mild face : Oft I had mused
Of calm and peace and deep forgetfulness,
Of folded hands, closed eyes, and heart at rest,
And slumber sound beneath a flowery turf,
Of faults forgotten, and an inner place
Kept sacred for us in the heart of friends ;
But these were idle fancies satisfied
With the mere husk of this great Mystery,
And dwelling in the outward shows of things.
Heaven is not mounted to on wings of dreams,
Nor doth the unthankful happiness of youth
Aim thitherward, but floats from bloom to bloom,
With earth's warm patch of sunshine well content :
'T is sorrow builds the shining ladder up
Whose golden rounds are our calamities,
Whereon our firm feet planting, nearer God
The spirit climbs, and hath its eyes unsealed.

True is it that Death's face seems stern and cold,
When he is sent to summon those we love,
But all God's angels come to us disguised ;
Sorrow and sickness, poverty and death,

One after other lift their frowning masks,
And we behold the seraph's face beneath,
All radiant with the glory and the calm
Of having looked upon the smile of God.
With every anguish of our earthly past
The spirit's sight grows clearer; this was meant
When Jesus touched the blind man's lids with clay.
Life is the jailer, Death the angel sent
To draw the unwilling bolts and set us free.
He flings not ope the ivory gate of Rest —
Only the fallen spirit knocks at that —
But to benigner regions beckons us,
To destinies of more rewarded toil.

In the hushed chamber, sitting by the dead,
It grates on us to hear the flood of life
Whirl rustling onward, senseless of our loss.
The bee hums on; around the blossomed vine
Whirs the light humming-bird; the cricket chirps;
The locust's shrill alarum stings the ear;
Hard by, the cock shouts lustily; from farm to farm,
His cheery brothers, telling of the sun,
Answer, till far away the joyance dies;
We never knew before how God had filled
The summer air with happy living sounds;
All round us seems an overplus of life,
And yet the one dear heart lies cold and still.
It is most strange, when the great Miracle
Hath for our sakes been done; when we have had
Our inwardest experience of God,
When with his presence still the room expands,

And is awed after him, that naught is changed,
That Nature's face looks unacknowledging,
And the mad world still dances heedless on
After its butterflies, and gives no sigh.
'T is hard at first to see it all aright;
In vain Faith blows her trump to summon back
Her scattered troop; yet, through the clouded glass
Of our own bitter tears, we learn to look
Undazzled on the kindness of God's face;
Earth is too dark, and Heaven alone shines through.

How changed, dear friend, are thy part and thy
    child's!
He bends above *thy* cradle now, or holds
His warning finger out to be thy guide;
Thou art the nursling now; he watches thee
Slow learning, one by one, the secret things
Which are to him used sights of every day;
He smiles to see thy wondering glances con
The grass and pebbles of the spirit world,
To thee miraculous; and he will teach
Thy knees their due observances of prayer.

Children are God's apostles, day by day,
Sent forth to preach of love, and hope, and peace;
Nor hath thy babe his mission left undone.
To me, at least, his going hence hath given
Serener thoughts and nearer to the skies,
And opened a new fountain in my heart
For thee, my friend, and all: and oh, if Death
More near approaches, meditates, and clasps

Even now some dearer, more reluctant hand,
God, strengthen thou my faith, that I may see
That 't is thine angel who, with loving haste,
Unto the service of the inner shrine
Doth waken thy belovèd with a kiss!

CAMBRIDGE, MASS., Sept. 3, 1844.

AN INCIDENT IN A RAILROAD CAR.

HE spoke of Burns : men rude and rough
   Pressed round to hear the praise of one
Whose breast was made of manly, simple stuff,
   As homespun as their own.

And, when he read, they forward leaned
   And heard, with eager hearts and ears,
His birdlike songs whom glory never weaned
   From humble smiles and tears.

Slowly there grew a tender awe,
   Sunlike o'er faces brown and hard,
As if in him who read they felt and saw
   Some presence of the bard.

It was a sight for sin and wrong,
   And slavish tyranny to see,
A sight to make our faith more pure and strong
   In high Humanity.

I thought, these men will carry hence,
   Promptings their former life above,
And something of a finer reverence
   For beauty, truth, and love.

God scatters love on every side,
   Freely among his children all,
And always hearts are lying open wide
   Wherein some grains may fall.

There is no wind but sows some seeds
   Of a more true and open life,
Which burst unlooked for into high-souled deeds
   With wayside beauty rife.

We find within these souls of ours
   Some wild germs of a higher birth,
Which in the poet's tropic heart bears flowers
   Whose fragrance fills the earth.

Within the hearts of all men lie
   These promises of wider bliss,
Which blossom into hopes that cannot die,
   In sunny hours like this.

All that hath been majestical
   In life or death since time began,
Is native in the simple heart of all,
   The angel heart of man.

And thus among the untaught poor
  Great deeds and feelings find a home
Which casts in shadow all the golden lore
  Of classic Greece or Rome.

Oh! mighty brother-soul of man,
  Where'er thou art, in low or high,
Thy skyey arches with exulting span
  O'er-roof infinity.

All thoughts that mould the age begin
  Deep down within the primitive soul,
And, from the many, slowly upward wing
  To One who grasps the whole.

In his broad breast, the feeling deep
  Which struggled on the many's tongue,
Swells to a tide of Thought whose surges leap
  O'er the weak throne of wrong.

Never did poesy appear
  So full of Heav'n to me as when
I saw how it would pierce through pride and fear,
  To lives of coarsest men.

It may be glorious to write
  Thoughts that shall glad the two or three
High souls like those far stars that come in sight
  Once in a century.

But better far it is to speak
   One simple word which now and then
Shall waken their free nature in the weak
   And friendless sons of men ;

To write some earnest verse or line
   Which, seeking not the praise of Art,
Shall make a clearer faith and manhood shine
   In the unlearnèd heart.

BOSTON, April, 1842.

AN INCIDENT OF THE FIRE AT HAMBURG.

THE tower of old Saint Nicholas soared upward to
   the skies,
Like some huge piece of nature's make, the growth
   of centuries ;
You could not deem its crowding spires a work of
   human art,
They seemed to struggle lightward so from a sturdy
   living heart.

Not Nature's self more freely speaks in crystal or in
   oak
Than, through the pious builder's hand, in that gray
   pile she spoke ;
And as from acorn springs the oak, so, freely and
   alone,
Sprang from his heart this hymn to God, sung in
   obedient stone.

It seemed a wondrous freak of chance, so perfect,
    yet so rough,
A whim of Nature crystallized slowly in granite tough ;
The thick spires yearned toward the sky in quaint
    harmonious lines,
And in broad sunlight basked and slept, like a grove
    of blasted pines.

Never did rock or stream or tree lay claim with better
    right
To all the adorning sympathies of shadow and of light ;
And, in that forest petrified, as forester there dwells
Stout Herman, the old sacristan, sole lord of all its
    bells.

Surge leaping after surge, the fire roared onward, red
    as blood,
Till half of Hamburg lay engulfed beneath the
    eddying flood ;
For miles away, the fiery spray poured down its
    deadly rain,
And back and forth the billows drew, and paused,
    and broke again.

From square to square, with tiger leaps, still on and
    on it came ;
The air to leeward trembled with the pantings of the
    flame,
And church and palace, which even now stood
    whelmed but to the knee,
Lift their black roofs like breakers lone amid the
    rushing sea.

Up in his tower old Herman sat and watched with
    quiet look ;
His soul had trusted God too long to be at last
    forsook :
He could not fear, for surely God a pathway would
    unfold
Through this red sea, for faithful hearts, as once he
    did of old.

But scarcely can he cross himself, or on his good
    saint call,
Before the sacrilegious flood o'erleaped the church-
    yard wall,
And, ere a *pater* half was said, 'mid smoke and
    crackling glare,
His island tower scarce juts its head above the wide
    despair.

Upon the peril's desperate peak his heart stood up
    sublime ;
His first thought was for God above, his next was
    for his chime ;
" Sing now, and make your voices heard in hymns
    of praise," cried he,
" As did the Israelites of old, safe-walking through
    the sea !

" Through this red sea our God hath made our path-
    way safe to shore ;
Our promised land stands full in sight ; shout now
    as ne'er before."

And, as the tower came crashing down, the bells, in
    clear accord,
Pealed forth the grand old German hymn — " All
    good souls praise the Lord ! "

SONNETS.

ON READING WORDSWORTH'S SONNETS IN DEFENCE OF CAPITAL
PUNISHMEN

I.

As the broad ocean endlessly upheaveth,
  With the majestic beating of his heart,
  The mighty tides, whereof its rightful part
Each sea-wide gulf and little weed receiveth —
So, through his soul who earnestly believeth
  Life from the universal Heart doth flow,
  Whereby some conquest of the eternal woe
By instinct of God's nature he achieveth :
A fuller pulse of this all-powerful Beauty
  Into the poet's gulf-like heart doth tide,
And he more keenly feels the glorious duty
  Of serving Truth despised and crucified —
Happy, unknowing sect or creed, to rest
And feel God flow forever through his breast.

II.

Once hardly in a cycle blossometh
  A flower-like soul ripe with the seeds of song,

A spirit foreordained to cope with wrong,
Whose divine thoughts are natural as breath,
Who the old Darkness thickly scattereth
　With starry words which shoot prevailing light
　Into the deeps, and wither with the blight
Of serene Truth the coward heart of Death:
Woe if such spirit sell his birthright high,
　And mock with lies the longing soul of man!
Yet one age longer must true Culture lie,
　Soothing her bitter fetters as she can,
Until new messages of love outstart
At the next beating of the infinite Heart.

III.

The love of all things springs from love of one;
　Wider the soul's horizon hourly grows,
　And over it with fuller glory flows
The sky-like spirit of God; a hope begun
In doubt and darkness, 'neath a fairer sun
　Cometh to fruitage, if it be of Truth;
　And to the law of meekness, faith, and ruth,
By inward sympathy shall all be won:
This thou shouldst know, who from the painted
　　feature
　Of shifting Fashion, couldst thy brethren turn
Unto the love of ever youthful nature,
　And of a beauty fadeless and eterne;
And always 't is the saddest sight to see
An old man faithless in Humanity.

IV.

A poet cannot strive for despotism;
　　His harp falls shattered; for it still must be
　　The instinct of great spirits to be free,
And the sworn foes of cunning barbarism.
He who has deepest searched the wide abysm
　　Of that life-giving Soul which men call fate,
　　Knows that to put more faith in lies and hate
Than truth and love, is the worst atheism:
Upward the soul forever turns her eyes;
　　The next hour always shames the hour before;
One beauty at its highest prophesies
　　That by whose side it shall seem mean and poor;
No Godlike thing knows aught of less and less,
But widens to the boundless Perfectness.

V.

Therefore think not the Past is wise alone,
　　For Yesterday knows nothing of the Best,
　　And thou shalt love it only as the nest
Whence glory-winged things to Heaven have flown.
To the great Soul alone are all things known,
　　Present and future are to her as past,
　　While she in glorious madness doth forecast
That perfect bud which seems a flower full-blown
To each new Prophet, and yet always opes
　　Fuller and fuller with each day and hour,
Heartening the soul with odor of fresh hopes,
　　And longings high and gushings of wide power;
Yet never is or shall be fully blown
Save in the forethought of the Eternal One.

VI.

Far 'yond this narrow parapet of Time,
    With eyes uplift, the poet's soul should look
    Into the Endless Promise, nor should brook
One prying doubt to shake his faith sublime;
To him the earth is ever in her prime
    And dewiness of morning; he can see
    Good lying hid, from all eternity,
Within the teeming womb of sin and crime;
His soul shall not be cramped by any bar —
    His nobleness should be so Godlike high
That his least deed is perfect as a star,
    His common look majestic as the sky,
And all o'erflooded with a light from far,
Undimmed by clouds of weak mortality.

BOSTON, April 2, 1842.

HAKON'S LAY.

THEN Thorstein looked at Hakon, where he sate,
Mute as a cloud amid the stormy hall,
And said: "O, Skald, sing now an olden song,
Such as our fathers heard who led great lives;
And, as the bravest on a shield is borne
Along the waving host that shouts him king,
So rode their thrones upon the thronging seas!"

Then the old man arose, white-haired he stood,
White-bearded, and with eyes that looked afar
From their still region of perpetual snow,
Over the little smokes and stirs of men:
His head was bowed with gathered flakes of years,
As winter bends the sea-foreboding pine,
But something triumphed in his brow and eye,
Which whoso saw it, could not see and crouch:
Loud rang the emptied beakers as he mused,
Brooding his eyried thoughts; then, as an eagle
Circles smooth-winged above the wind-vexed woods,
So wheeled his soul into the air of song
High o'er the stormy hall; and thus he sang:

" The fletcher for his arrow-shaft picks out
Wood closest-grained, long-seasoned, straight as
      light;
And, from a quiver full of such as these,
The wary bow-man, matched against his peers,
Long doubting, singles yet once more the best.
Who is it that can make such shafts as Fate?
What archer of his arrows is so choice,
Or hits the white so surely? They are men,
The chosen of her quiver; nor for her
Will every reed suffice, or cross-grained stick
At random from life's vulgar fagot plucked:
Such answer household ends; but she will have
Souls straight and clear, of toughest fibre, sound
Down to the heart of heart; from these she strips
All needless stuff, all sapwood, hardens them,

From circumstance untoward feathers plucks
Crumpled and cheap, and barbs with iron will:
The hour that passes is her quiver-boy;
When she draws bow, 't is not across the wind,
Nor 'gainst the sun, her haste-snatched arrow
      sings,
For sun and wind have plighted faith to her:
Ere men have heard the sinew twang, behold,
In the butt's heart her trembling messenger!

" The song is old and simple that I sing:
Good were the days of yore, when men were tried
By ring of shields, as now by ring of gold;
But, while the gods are left, and hearts of men
And the free ocean, still the days are good;
Through the broad Earth roams Opportunity
And knocks at every door of hut or hall,
Until she finds the brave soul that she wants."

He ceased, and instantly the frothy tide
Of interrupted wassail roared along;
But Leif, the son of Eric, sate apart
Musing, and, with his eyes upon the fire,
Saw shapes of arrows, lost as soon as seen;
But then with that resolve his heart was bent,
Which, like a humming shaft, through many a strife
Of day and night across the unventured seas,
Shot the brave prow to cut on Vinland sands
The first rune in the Saga of the West.

TO THE FUTURE.

O, LAND of Promise! from what Pisgah's height
  Can I behold thy stretch of peaceful bowers?
Thy golden harvests flowing out of sight,
  Thy nestled homes and sun-illumined towers?
Gazing upon the sunset's high-heaped gold,
  Its crags of opal and of chrysolite,
Its deeps on deeps of glory that unfold
      Still brightening abysses,
      And blazing precipices,
Whence but a scanty leap it seems to heaven,
      Sometimes a glimpse is given,
Of thy more gorgeous realm, thy more unstinted
      blisses.

O, Land of Quiet! to thy shore the surf
  Of the perturbed Present rolls and sleeps;
Our storms breathe soft as June upon thy turf
  And lure out blossoms; to thy bosom leaps,
As to a mother's, the o'er-wearied heart,
Hearing far off and dim the toiling mart,
      The hurrying feet, the curses without number,
      And, circled with the glow Elysian,
      Of thine exulting vision,
Out of its very cares wooes charms for peace and
      slumber.

To thee the Earth lifts up her fettered hands
  And cries for vengeance; with a pitying smile
Thou blessest her, and she forgets her bands,

And her old woe-worn face a little while
Grows young and noble; unto thee the Oppressor
    Looks, and is dumb with awe;
    The eternal law
Which makes the crime its own blindfold redresser,
  Shadows his heart with perilous foreboding,
    And he can see the grim-eyed Doom
    From out the trembling gloom
Its silent-footed steeds toward his palace goading.

What promises hast thou for Poet's eyes,
  Aweary of the turmoil and the wrong!
To all their hopes what over-joyed replies!
  What undreamed ecstasies for blissful song!
Thy happy plains no war-trump's brawling clangor
  Disturbs, and fools the poor to hate the poor;
The humble glares not on the high with anger;
  Love leaves no grudge at less, no greed for more;
In vain strives Self the godlike sense to smother;
    From the soul's deeps
    It throbs and leaps;
The noble 'neath foul rags beholds his long-lost
    brother.

To thee the Martyr looketh, and his fires
  Unlock their fangs and leave his spirit free;
To thee the Poet mid his toil aspires,
  And grief and hunger climb about his knee
Welcome as children; thou upholdest
  The lone Inventor by his demon haunted;
The Prophet cries to thee when hearts are coldest,

And, gazing o'er the midnight's bleak abyss,
   Sees the drowsed soul awaken at thy kiss,
And stretch its happy arms and leap up disen-
      chanted.

Thou bringest vengeance, but so loving kindly
   The guilty thinks it pity; taught by thee
Fierce tyrants drop the scourges wherewith blindly
    Their own souls they were scarring; conquerors
      see
With horror in their hands the accursed spear
   That tore the meek One's side on Calvary,
And from their trophies shrink with ghastly fear;
   Thou, too, art the Forgiver,
The beauty of man's soul to man revealing;
   The arrows from thy quiver
Pierce error's guilty heart, but only pierce for healing.

O, whither, whither, glory-wingèd dreams,
   From out Life's sweat and turmoil would ye bear
      me?
Shut, gates of Fancy, on your golden gleams,
   This agony of hopeless contrast spare me!
Fade, cheating glow, and leave me to my night!
      He is a coward who would borrow
      A charm against the present sorrow
From the vague Future's promise of delight:
   As life's alarums nearer roll,
      The ancestral buckler calls,
      Self-clanging, from the walls
   In the high temple of the soul;

Out of Doors.

Where are most sorrows, there the poet's sphere is,
    To feed the soul with patience,
    To heal its desolations
With words of unshorn truth, with love that never
    wearies.

OUT OF DOORS.

'T IS good to be abroad in the sun,
His gifts abide when day is done;
Each thing in nature from his cup
Gathers a several virtue up;
The grace within its being's reach
Becomes the nutriment of each,
And the same life imbibed by all
Makes each most individual:
Here the twig-bending peaches seek
The glow that mantles in their cheek —
Hence comes the Indian-summer bloom
That hazes round the basking plum,
And, from the same impartial light,
The grass sucks green, the lily white.

Like these the soul, for sunshine made,
Grows wan and gracile in the shade,
Her faculties, which God decreed
Various as Summer's dædal breed,
With one sad color are imbued,
Shut from the sun that tints their blood;
The shadow of the poet's roof

Deadens the dyes of warp and woof;
Whate'er of ancient song remains
Has fresh air flowing in its veins,
For Greece and eldest Ind knew well
That out of doors, with world-wide swell
Arches the student's lawful cell.

Away, unfruitful lore of books,
For whose vain idiom we reject
The spirit's mother-dialect,
Aliens among the birds and brooks,
Dull to interpret or believe
What gospels lost the woods retrieve,
Or what the eves-dropping violet
Reports from God, who walketh yet
His garden in the hush of eve!
Away, ye pedants city-bred,
Unwise of heart, too wise of head,
Who handcuff Art with *thus and so,*
And in each other's footprints tread,
Like those who walk through drifted snow;

Who, from deep study of brick walls
Conjecture of the water-falls,
By six square feet of smoke-stained sky
Compute those deeps that overlie
The still tarn's heaven-anointed eye,
And, in your earthen crucible,
With chemic tests essay to spell
How nature works in field and dell!
Seek we where Shakspeare buried gold?

Such hands no charmed witch-hazel hold;
To beach and rock repeats the sea
The mystic *Open Sesame*;
Old Greylock's voices not in vain
Comment on Milton's mountain strain,
And cunningly the various wind
Spenser's locked music can unbind.

A REVERIE.

IN the twilight deep and silent
Comes thy spirit unto mine,
When the moonlight and the starlight
Over cliff and woodland shine,
And the quiver of the river
Seems a thrill of joy benign.

Then I rise and wander slowly
To the headland by the sea,
When the evening star throbs setting
Through the cloudy cedar-tree,
And from under, mellow thunder
Of the surf comes fitfully.

Then within my soul I feel thee
Like a gleam of other years,
Visions of my childhood murmur
Their old madness in my ears,
Till the pleasance of thy presence
Cools my heart with blissful tears.

All the wondrous dreams of boyhood —
All youth's fiery thirst of praise —
All the surer hopes of manhood
Blossoming in sadder days —
Joys that bound me, griefs that crowned me
With a better wreath than bays —

All the longings after freedom —
The vague love of human kind,
Wandering far and near at random
Like a winged seed in the wind —
The dim yearnings and fierce burnings
Of an undirected mind —

All of these, oh best belovèd,
Happiest present dreams and past,
In thy love find safe fulfilment,
Ripened into truths at last;
Faith and beauty, hope and duty
To one centre gather fast.

How my nature, like an ocean,
At the breath of thine awakes,
Leaps its shores in mad exulting
And in foamy thunder breaks,
Then downsinking, lieth shrinking
At the tumult that it makes!

Blazing Hesperus hath sunken
Low within the pale-blue west,
And with golden splendor crowneth

The horizon's piny crest;
Thoughtful quiet stills the riot
Of wild longing in my breast.

Home I loiter through the moonlight,
Underneath the quivering trees,
Which, as if a spirit stirred them,
Sway and bend, till by degrees
The far surge's murmur merges
In the rustle of the breeze.

———

IN SADNESS.

THERE is not in this life of ours
    One bliss unmixed with fears;
The hope that wakes our deepest powers
    A face of sadness wears,
And the dew that showers our dearest flowers
    Is the bitter dew of tears.

Fame waiteth long, and lingereth
    Through weary nights and morns—
And evermore the shadow Death
    With mocking finger scorns
That underneath the laurel wreath
    Should be a wreath of thorns.

The laurel leaves are cool and green,
  But the thorns are hot and sharp,
Lean Hunger grins and stares between
  The poet and his harp;
Though of Love's sunny sheen his woof have been,
  Grim Want thrusts in the warp.

And if beyond this darksome clime
  Some fair star Hope may see,
That keeps unjarred the blissful chime
  Of its golden infancy —
Where the harvest-time of faith sublime
  Not always is to be —

Yet would the true soul rather choose
  Its home where sorrow is,
Than in a sated peace to lose
  Its life's supremest bliss —
The rainbow hues that bend profuse
  O'er cloudy spheres like this —

The want, the sorrow and the pain,
  That are Love's right to cure —
The sunshine bursting after rain —
  The gladness insecure
That makes us fain strong hearts to gain,
  To do and to endure.

High natures must be thunder-scarred
  With many a searing wrong;
From mother Sorrow's breasts the bard

Sucks gifts of deepest song,
Nor all unmarred with struggles hard
Wax the Soul's sinews strong.

Dear Patience, too, is born of woe,
Patience that opes the gate
Wherethrough the soul of man must go
Up to each nobler state,
Whose voice's flow so meek and low
Smooths the bent brows of Fate.

Though Fame be slow, yet Death is swift,
And, o'er the spirit's eyes,
Life after life doth change and shift
With larger destinies:
As on we drift, some wider rift
Shows us serener skies.

And though naught falleth to us here
But gains the world counts loss,
Though all we hope of wisdom clear
When climbed to seems but dross,
Yet all, though ne'er Christ's faith they wear,
At least may share his cross.

————

FAREWELL.

FAREWELL! as the bee round the blossom
Doth murmur drowsily,
So murmureth round my bosom
The memory of thee;

Lingering, it seems to go,
When the wind more full doth flow,
Waving the flower to and fro,
But still returneth, Marian !
My hope no longer burneth,
Which did so fiercely burn,
My joy to sorrow turneth,
Although loath, loath to turn —
I would forget —
And yet — and yet
My heart to thee still yearneth, Marian !

Fair as a single star thou shinest,
And white as lilies are
The slender hands wherewith thou twinest
Thy heavy auburn hair ;
Thou art to me
A memory
Of all that is divinest :
Thou art so fair and tall,
Thy looks so queenly are,
Thy very shadow on the wall,
Thy step upon the stair,
The thought that thou art nigh,
The chance look of thine eye
Are more to me than all, Marian,
And will be till I die !

As the last quiver of a bell
Doth fade into the air,
With a subsiding swell

That dies we know not where,
So my hope melted and was gone:
I raised mine eyes to bless the star
That shared its light with me so far
Below its silver throne,
And gloom and chilling vacancy
Were all was left to me,
In the dark, bleak night I was alone!
Alone in the blessed Earth, Marian,
For what were all to me —
Its love, and light, and mirth, Marian,
If I were not with thee?

My heart will not forget thee
More than the moaning brine
Forgets the moon when she is set;
The gush when first I met thee
That thrilled my brain like wine,
Doth thrill as madly yet;
My heart cannot forget thee,
Though it may droop and pine,
Too deeply it had set thee
In every love of mine;
No new moon ever cometh,
No flower ever bloometh,
No twilight ever gloometh
But I 'm more only thine.
Oh look not on me, Marian,
Thine eyes are wild and deep,
And they have won me, Marian,

From peacefulness and sleep;
The sunlight doth not sun me,
The meek moonshine doth shun me,
All sweetest voices stun me —
There is no rest
Within my breast
And I can only weep, Marian!

As a landbird far at sea
Doth wander through the sleet
And drooping downward wearily
Finds no rest for her feet,
So wandereth my memory
O'er the years when we did meet:
I used to say that everything
Partook a share of thee,
That not a little bird could sing,
Or green leaf flutter on a tree,
That nothing could be beautiful
Save part of thee were there,
That from thy soul so clear and full
All bright and blessèd things did cull
The charm to make them fair;
And now I know
That it was so,
Thy spirit through the earth doth flow
And face me whereso'er I go —
What right hath perfectness to give
Such weary weight of woe
Unto the soul which cannot live

On anything more low?
Oh leave me, leave me, Marian,
There 's no fair thing I see
But doth deceive me, Marian,
Into sad dreams of thee !

A cold snake gnaws my heart
And crushes round my brain,
And I should glory but to part
So bitterly again,
Feeling the slow tears start
And fall in fiery rain :
There's a wide ring round the moon,
The ghost-like clouds glide by,
And I hear the sad winds croon
A dirge to the lowering sky ;
There 's nothing soft or mild
In the pale moon's sickly light,
But all looks strange and wild
Through the dim, foreboding night :
I think thou must be dead
In some dark and lonely place,
With candles at thy head,
And a pall above thee spread
To hide thy dead, cold face ;
But I can see thee underneath
So pale, and still, and fair,
Thine eyes closed smoothly and a wreath
Of flowers in thy hair ;
I never saw thy face so clear
When thou wast with the living,

As now beneath the pall, so drear,
And stiff, and unforgiving;
I cannot flee thee, Marian,
I cannot turn away,
Mine eyes must see thee, Marian,
Through salt tears night and day.

————

A DIRGE.

POET! lonely is thy bed,
And the turf is overhead—
　　Cold earth is thy cover;
But thy heart hath found release,
And it slumbers full of peace
'Neath the rustle of green trees
And the warm hum of the bees,
　　'Mid the drowsy clover;
Through thy chamber, still as death,
A smooth gurgle wandereth,
As the blue stream murmureth
　　To the blue sky over.
Three paces from the silver strand,
Gently in the fine, white sand,
With a lily in thy hand,
　　Pale as snow, they laid thee;
In no coarse earth wast thou hid,
And no gloomy coffin-lid
　　Darkly overweighed thee.

Silently as snow-flakes drift,
The smooth sand did sift and sift
   O'er the bed they made thee;
All sweet birds did come and sing
At thy sunny burying—
   Choristers unbidden,
And, beloved of sun and dew,
Meek forget-me-nots upgrew
Where thine eyes so large and blue
   'Neath the turf were hidden.

Where thy stainless clay doth lie,
Blue and open is the sky,
And the white clouds wander by,
Dreams of summer silently
   Darkening the river;
Thou hearest the clear water run;
And the ripples every one,
Scattering the golden sun,
   Through thy silence quiver;
Vines trail down upon the stream,
Into its smooth and glassy dream
   A green stillness spreading,
And the shiner, perch, and bream
Through the shadowed waters gleam
   'Gainst the current heading.

White as snow, thy winding sheet
Shelters thee from head to feet,
   Save thy pale face only;
Thy face is turned toward the skies,

The lids lie meekly o'er thine eyes,
And the low-voiced pine-tree sighs
    O'er thy bed so lonely.
All thy life thou lov'dst its shade:
Underneath it thou art laid,
    In an endless shelter;
Thou hearest it forever sigh
As the wind's vague longings die
In its branches dim and high —
Thou hear'st the waters gliding by
    Slumberously welter.

Thou wast full of love and truth,
Of forgiveness and ruth —
Thy great heart with hope and youth
    Tided to o'erflowing.
Thou didst dwell in mysteries,
And there lingered on thine eyes
Shadows of serener skies,
Awfully wild memories,
    That were like foreknowing;
Through the earth thou would'st have gone,
Lighted from within alone,
Seeds from flowers in Heaven grown
    With a free hand sowing.

Thou didst remember well and long
Some fragments of thine angel-song,
And strive, through want of woe and wrong,
    To win the world unto it;
Thy sin it was to see and hear

Beyond To-day's dim hemisphere —
Beyond all mists of hope and fear,
Into a life more true and clear,
   And dearly thou didst rue it;
Light of the new world thou hadst won,
O'erflooded by a purer sun —
Slowly Fate's ship came drifting on,
And through the dark, save thou, not one
   Caught of the land a token.
Thou stood'st upon the farthest prow,
Something within thy soul said " Now! "
And leaping forth with eager brow,
   Thou fell'st on shore heart-broken.

Long time thy brethren stood in fear;
Only the breakers far and near,
White with their anger, they could hear;
The sounds of land, which thy quick ear
   Caught long ago, they heard not.
And, when at last they reached the strand,
They found thee lying on the sand
With some wild flowers in thy hand,
   But thy cold bosom stirred not;
They listened, but they heard no sound
Save from the glad life all around
   A low, contented murmur.
The long grass flowed adown the hill,
A hum rose from a hidden rill,
But thy glad heart, that knew no ill
But too much love, lay dead and still —
The only thing that sent a chill
   Into the heart of summer.

Thou didst not seek the poet's wreath
   But too soon didst win it;
Without 't was green, but underneath
Were scorn and loneliness and death,
Gnawing the brain with burning teeth,
   And making mock within it.
Thou, who wast full of nobleness,
Whose very life-blood 't was to bless,
   Whose soul's one law was giving,
Must bandy words with wickedness,
Haggle with hunger and distress,
To win that death which worldliness
   Calls bitterly a living.

"Thou sow'st no gold, and shalt not reap!"
Muttered earth, turning in her sleep;
"Come home to the Eternal Deep!"
Murmured a voice, and a wide sweep
Of wings through thy soul's hush did creep,
   As of thy doom o'erflying;
It seemed that thy strong heart would leap
Out of thy breast, and thou didst weep,
   But not with fear of dying;
Men could not fathom thy deep fears,
They could not understand thy tears,
The hoarded agony of years
   Of bitter self-denying.
So once, when high above the spheres
Thy spirit sought its starry peers,
It came not back to face the jeers
   Of brothers who denied it;

Star-crowned, thou dost possess the deeps
Of God, and thy white body sleeps
Where the lone pine forever keeps
   Patient watch beside it.

Poet! underneath the turf,
   Soft thou sleepest, free from morrow,
Thou hast struggled through the surf
   Of wild thoughts and want and sorrow.
Now, beneath the moaning pine,
   Full of rest, thy body lieth,
While far up is clear sunshine,
Underneath a sky divine,
   Her loosed wings thy spirit trieth;
Oft she strove to spread them here,
But they were too white and clear
For our dingy atmosphere.

Thy body findeth ample room
In its still and grassy tomb
   By the silent river;
But thy spirit found the earth
Narrow for the mighty birth
   Which it dreamed of ever;
Thou wast guilty of a rhyme
Learned in a benigner clime,
And of that more grievous crime,
An ideal too sublime
For the low-hung sky of Time.

The calm spot where thy body lies
Gladdens thy soul in Paradise,
   It is so still and holy;
Thy body sleeps serenely there,
And well for it thy soul may care,
It was so beautiful and fair,
   Lily white so wholly.
From so pure and sweet a frame
Thy spirit parted as it came,
   Gentle as a maiden;
Now it lieth full of rest —
Sods are lighter on its breast
Than the great, prophetic guest
   Wherewith it was laden.

FANCIES ABOUT A ROSEBUD,

PRESSED IN AN OLD COPY OF SPENSER.

Who prest you here? The Past can tell,
  When summer skies were bright above,
And some full heart did leap and swell
  Beneath the white new moon of love.

Some Poet, haply, when the world
  Showed like a calm sea, grand and blue,
Ere its cold, inky waves had curled
  O'er the numb heart once warm and true;

When, with his soul brimful of morn,
  He looked beyond the vale of Time,
Nor saw therein the dullard scorn
  That made his heavenliness a crime;

When, musing o'er the Poets olden,
  His soul did like a sun upstart
To shoot its arrows, clear and golden,
  Through slavery's cold and darksome heart.

Alas! too soon the veil is lifted
  That hangs between the soul and pain,
Too soon the morning-red hath drifted
  Into dull cloud, or fallen in rain!

Or were you prest by one who nurst
  Bleak memories of love gone by,
Whose heart, like a star fallen, burst
  In dark and erring vacancy?

To him you still were fresh and green
  As when you grew upon the stalk,
And many a breezy summer scene
  Came back — and many a moonlit walk;

And there would be a hum of bees,
  A smell of childhood in the air,
And old, fresh feelings cooled the breeze
  That, like loved fingers, stirred his hair!

Then would you suddenly be blasted
   By the keen wind of one dark thought,
One nameless woe, that had outlasted
   The sudden blow whereby 't was brought.

Or were you prest here by two lovers
   Who seemed to read these verses rare,
But found between the antique covers
   What Spenser could not prison there:

Songs which his glorious soul had heard,
   But his dull pen could never write,
Which flew, like some gold-wingèd bird,
   Through the blue heaven out of sight?

My heart is with them as they sit,
   I see the rosebud in her breast,
I see her small hand taking it
   From out its odorous, snowy nest;

I hear him swear that he will keep it,
   In memory of that blessed day,
To smile on it or over-weep it
   When she and spring are far away.

Ah me! I needs must droop my head,
   And brush away a happy tear,
For they are gone, and, dry and dead,
   The rosebud lies before me here.

Yet is it in no stranger's hand,
　For I will guard it tenderly,
And it shall be a magic wand
　To bring mine own true love to me.

My heart runs o'er with sweet surmises,
　The while my fancy weaves her rhyme,
Kind hopes and musical surprises
　Throng round me from the olden time.

I do not care to know who prest you:
　Enough for me to feel and know
That some heart's love and longing blest you,
　Knitting to-day with long-ago.

NEW YEAR'S EVE, 1844.

A FRAGMENT.

THE night is calm and beautiful; the snow
Sparkles beneath the clear and frosty moon
And the cold stars, as if it took delight
In its own silent whiteness; the hushed earth
Sleeps in the soft arms of the embracing blue,
Secure as if angelic squadrons yet
Encamped about her, and each watching star
Gained double brightness from the flashing arms
Of wingèd and unsleeping sentinels.
Upward the calm of infinite silence deepens,

The sea that flows between high heaven and earth,
Musing by whose smooth brink we sometimes find
A stray leaf floated from those happier shores,
And hope, perchance not vainly, that some flower,
Which we had watered with our holiest tears,
Pale blooms, and yet our scanty garden's best,
O'er the same ocean piloted by love,
May find a haven at the feet of God,
And be not wholly worthless in his sight.
O, high dependence on a higher Power,
Sole stay for all these restless faculties
That wander, Ishmael-like, the desert bare
Wherein our human knowledge hath its home,
Shifting their light-framed tents from day to day,
With each new-found oasis, wearied soon,
And only certain of uncertainty!
O, mighty humbleness that feels with awe,
Yet with a vast exulting feels, no less,
That this huge Minster of the Universe,
Whose smallest oratories are glorious worlds,
With painted oriels of dawn and sunset;
Whose carvèd ornaments are systems grand,
Orion kneeling in his starry niche,
The Lyre whose strings give music audible
To holy ears, and countless splendors more,
Crowned by the blazing Cross high-hung o'er all;
Whose organ music is the solemn stops
Of endless Change breathed through by endless
      Good;
Whose choristers are all the morning stars;
Whose altar is the sacred human heart

Whereon Love's candles burn unquenchably,
Trimmed day and night by gentle-handed Peace ;
With all its arches and its pinnacles
That stretch forever and forever up,
Is founded on the silent heart of God,
Silent, yet pulsing forth exhaustless life
Through the least veins of all created things.
Fit musings these for the departing year ;
And God be thanked for such a crystal night
As fills the spirit with good store of thoughts,
That, like a cheering fire of walnut, crackle
Upon the hearthstone of the heart, and cast
A mild home-glow o'er all Humanity !
Yes, though the poisoned shafts of evil doubts
Assail the skyey panoply of Faith,
Though the great hopes which we have had for man,
Foes in disguise, because they based belief
On man's endeavor, not on God's decree —
Though these proud-visaged hopes, once turned to
    fly,
Hurl backward many a deadly Parthian dart
That rankles in the soul and makes it sick
With vain regret, nigh verging on despair —
Yet, in such calm and earnest hours as this,
We well can feel how every living heart
That sleeps to-night in palace or in cot,
Or unroofed hovel, or which need hath known
Of other homestead than the arching sky,
Is circled watchfully with seraph fires ;
How our own erring will it is that hangs
The flaming sword o'er Eden's unclosed gate,

Which gives free entrance to the pure in heart,
And with its guarding walls doth fence the meek.
Sleep then, O Earth, in thy blue-vaulted cradle,
Bent over always by thy mother Heaven!
We all are tall enough to reach God's hand,
And angels are no taller: looking back
Upon the smooth wake of a year o'erpast,
We see the black clouds furling, one by one,
From the advancing majesty of Truth,
And something won for Freedom, whose least gain
Is as a firm and rock-built citadel
Wherefrom to launch fresh battle on her foes;
Or, leaning from the time's extremest prow,
If we gaze forward through the blinding spray,
And dimly see how much of ill remains,
How many fetters to be sawn asunder
By the slow toil of individual zeal,
Or haply rusted by salt tears in twain,
We feel, with something of a sadder heart,
Yet bracing up our bruisèd mail the while,
And fronting the old foe with fresher spirit,
How great it is to breathe with human breath,
To be but poor foot-soldiers in the ranks
Of our old exiled king, Humanity;
Encamping after every hard-won field
Nearer and nearer Heaven's happy plains.

Many great souls have gone to rest, and sleep
Under this armor, free and full of peace:
If these have left the earth, yet Truth remains,
Endurance, too, the crowning faculty

Of noble minds, and Love, invincible
By any weapons ; and these hem us round
With silence such that all the groaning clank
Of this mad engine men have made of earth
Dulls not some ears for catching purer tones,
That wander from the dim surrounding vast,
Or far more clear melodious prophecies,
The natural music of the heart of man,
Which by kind Sorrow's ministry hath learned
That the true sceptre of all power is love,
And humbleness the palace-gate of truth.
What man with soul so blind as sees not here
The first faint tremble of Hope's morning-star,
Foretelling how the God-forged shafts of dawn,
Fitted already on their golden string,
Shall soon leap earthward with exulting flight
To thrid the dark heart of that evil faith
Whose trust is in the clumsy arms of Force,
The ozier hauberk of a ruder age?
Freedom ! thou other name for happy Truth,
Thou warrior-maid, whose steel-clad feet were never
Out of the stirrup, nor thy lance uncouched,
Nor thy fierce eye enticèd from its watch,
Thou hast learned now, by hero-blood in vain
Poured to enrich the soil which tyrants reap ;
By wasted lives of prophets, and of those
Who, by the promise in their souls upheld,
Into the red arms of a fiery death
Went blithely as the golden-girdled bee
Sinks in the sleepy poppy's cup of flame
By the long woes of nations set at war,

That so the swollen torrent of their wrath
May find a vent, else sweeping off like straws
The thousand cobweb threads, grown cable-huge
By time's long gathered dust, but cobwebs still,
Which bind the Many that the Few may gain
Leisure to wither by the drought of ease
What heavenly germs in their own souls were
    sown ; —
By all these searching lessons thou hast learned
To throw aside thy blood-stained helm and spear
And with thy bare brow daunt the enemy's front,
Knowing that God will make the lily stalk,
In the soft grasp of naked Gentleness,
Stronger than iron spear to shatter through
The sevenfold toughness of Wrong's idle shield.

A MYSTICAL BALLAD.

I.

THE sunset scarce had dimmed away
Into the twilight's doubtful gray :
One long cloud o'er the horizon lay,
'Neath which, a streak of bluish white,
Wavered between the day and night ;
Over the pine-trees on the hill
The trembling evening-star did thrill,
And the new moon, with slender rim,
Through the elm arches gleaming dim,
Filled memory's chalice to the brim.

II.

On such an eve the heart doth grow
Full of surmise, and scarce can know
If it be now or long ago,
Or if indeed it doth exist; —
A wonderful enchanted mist
From the new moon doth wander out,
Wrapping all things in mystic doubt,
So that this world doth seem untrue,
And all our fancies to take hue
From some life ages since gone through.

III.

The maiden sat and heard the flow
Of the west wind so soft and low
The leaves scarce quivered to and fro;
Unbound, her heavy golden hair
Rippled across her bosom bare,
Which gleamed with thrilling snowy white
Far through the magical moonlight:
The breeze rose with a rustling swell,
And from afar there came the smell
Of a long-forgotten lily-bell.

IV.

The dim moon rested on the hill,
But silent, without thought or will,
Where sat the dreamy maiden still;
And now the moon's tip, like a star,

Drew down below the horizon's bar;
To her black noon the night hath grown,
Yet still the maiden sits alone,
Pale as a corpse beneath a stream,
And her white bosom still doth gleam
Through the deep midnight like a dream.

V

Cloudless the morning came and fair,
And lavishly the sun doth share
His gold among her golden hair,
Kindling it all, till slowly so
A glory round her head doth glow;
A withered flower is in her hand,
That grew in some far distant land,
And, silently transfigurèd,
With wide calm eyes, and undrooped head,
They found the stranger-maiden dead.

VI.

A youth, that morn, 'neath other skies,
Felt sudden tears burn in his eyes,
And his heart throng with memories;
All things without him seemed to win
Strange brotherhood with things within,
And he forever felt that he
Walked in the midst of mystery,
And thenceforth, why, he could not tell,
His heart would curdle at the smell
Of his once-cherished lily-bell.

VII.

Something from him had passed away;
Some shifting trembles of clear day,
Through starry crannies in his clay,
Grew bright and steadfast, more and more,
Where all had been dull earth before;
And, through these chinks, like him of old,
His spirit converse high did hold
With clearer loves and wider powers,
That brought him dewy fruits and flowers
From far Elysian groves and bowers.

VIII.

Just on the farther bound of sense,
Unproved by outward evidence,
But known by a deep influence
Which through our grosser clay doth shine
With light unwaning and divine,
Beyond where highest thought can fly
Stretcheth the world of Mystery —
And they not greatly overween
Who deem that nothing true hath been
Save the unspeakable Unseen.

IX.

One step beyond life's work-day things,
One more beat of the soul's broad wings,
One deeper sorrow sometimes brings
The spirit into that great Vast
Where neither future is nor past;

None knoweth how he entered there,
But, waking, finds his spirit where
He thought an angel could not soar,
And, what he called false dreams before,
The very air about his door.

x.

These outward seemings are but shows
Whereby the body sees and knows;
Far down beneath, forever flows
A stream of subtlest sympathies
That make our spirits strangely wise
In awe, and fearful bodings dim
Which, from the sense's outer rim,
Stretch forth beyond our thought and sight,
Fine arteries of circling light,
Pulsed outward from the Infinite.

OPENING POEM TO

A YEAR'S LIFE.

Hope first the youthful Poet leads,
And he is glad to follow her;
Kind is she, and to all his needs
With a free hand doth minister.

But, when sweet Hope at last hath fled,
Cometh her sister, Memory;
She wreathes Hope's garlands round her head,
And strives to seem as fair as she.

Then Hope comes back, and by the hand
She leads a child most fair to see,
Who with a joyous face doth stand
Uniting Hope and Memory.

So brighter grew the Earth around,
And bluer grew the sky above;
The Poet now his guide hath found,
And follows in the steps of Love.

———

DEDICATION

TO VOLUME OF POEMS ENTITLED

A YEAR'S LIFE.

THE gentle Una I have loved,
The snowy maiden, pure and mild,
Since ever by her side I roved,
Through ventures strange, a wondering child,
In fantasy a Red Cross Knight,
Burning for her dear sake to fight.

If there be one who can, like her,
Make sunshine in life's shady places,
One in whose holy bosom stir
As many gentle household graces —
And such I think there needs must be —
Will she accept this book from me?

THRENODIA.

GONE, gone from us! and shall we see
Those sybil-leaves of destiny,
Those calm eyes, nevermore?
Those deep, dark eyes so warm and bright,
Wherein the fortunes of the man
Lay slumbering in prophetic light,
In characters a child might scan?
So bright, and gone forth utterly?
O stern word — Nevermore!

The stars of those two gentle eyes
Will shine no more on earth;
Quenched are the hopes that had their birth,
As we watched them slowly rise,
Stars of a mother's fate;
And she would read them o'er and o'er,
Pondering, as she sate,
Over their dear astrology,
Which she had conned and conned before,

Deeming she needs must read aright
What was writ so passing bright.
And yet, alas! she knew not why,
Her voice would falter in its song,
And tears would slide from out her eye,
Silent, as they were doing wrong.
Her heart was like a wind-flower, bent
Even to breaking with the balmy dew,
Turning its heavenly nourishment
(That filled with tears its eyes of blue,
Like a sweet suppliant that weeps in prayer,
Making her innocency show more fair,
 Albeit unwitting of the ornament,)
Into a load too great for it to bear:
O stern word — Nevermore!

   The tongue, that scarce had learned to claim
An entrance to a mother's heart
By that dear talisman, a mother's name,
Sleeps all forgetful of its art!
I loved to see the infant soul
(How mighty in the weakness
Of its untutored meekness!)
Peep timidly from out its nest,
His lips, the while,
Fluttering with half-fledged words,
Or hushing to a smile
That more than words expressed,
When his glad mother on him stole
And snatched him to her breast!
O, thoughts were brooding in those eyes,

That would have soared like strong-winged birds
Far, far into the skies,
Gladdening the earth with song
And gushing harmonies,
Had he but tarried with us long!
O stern word — Nevermore!

　　How peacefully they rest,
Crossfolded there
Upon his little breast,
Those small, white hands that ne'er were still before,
But ever sported with his mother's hair,
Or the plain cross that on her breast she wore!
Her heart no more will beat
To feel the touch of that soft palm,
That ever seemed a new surprise
Sending glad thoughts up to her eyes
To bless him with their holy calm —
Sweet thoughts! they made her eyes as sweet.
How quiet are the hands
That wove those pleasant bands!
But that they do not rise and sink
With his calm breathing, I should think
That he were dropped asleep;
Alas! too deep, too deep
In this his slumber!
Time scarce can number
The years ere he will wake again
O, may we see his eyelids open then!
O stern word — Nevermore!

As the airy gossamere,
Floating in the sunlight clear,
Where'er it toucheth clinging tightly
Round glossy leaf or stump unsightly,
So from his spirit wandered out
Tendrils spreading all about,
Knitting all things to its thrall
With a perfect love of all:
O stern word — Nevermore!

He did but float a little way
Adown the stream of time,
With dreamy eyes watching the ripples play,
Or listening to their fairy chime;
His slender sail
Ne'er felt the gale;
He did but float a little way,
And, putting to the shore
While yet 't was early day,
Went calmly on his way,
To dwell with us no more!
No jarring did he feel,
No grating on his vessel's keel;
A strip of silver sand
Mingled the waters with the land
Where he was seen no more:
O stern word — Nevermore!

Full short his journey was; no dust
Of earth unto his sandals clave;
The weary weight that old men must,

He bore not to the grave.
He seemed a cherub who had lost his way
And wandered hither, so his stay
With us was short, and 't was most meet
That he should be no delver in Earth's clod,
Nor need to pause and cleanse his feet
To stand before his God ;
O blest word — Evermore !

THE SERENADE.

GENTLE, Lady, be thy sleeping,
Peaceful may thy dreamings be,
While around thy soul is sweeping,
Dreamy-winged, our melody ;
Chant we, Brothers, sad and slow,
Let our song be soft and low
As the voice of other years,
Let our hearts within us melt,
To gentleness, as if we felt
The dropping of our mother's tears.

Lady ! now our song is bringing
Back again thy childhood's hours —
Hearest thou the humbee singing
Drowsily among the flowers ?
Sleepily, sleepily
In the noontide swayeth he,

Half rested on the slender stalks
That edge those well-known garden walks;
Hearest thou the fitful whirring
Of the humbird's viewless wings —
Feel'st not round thy heart the stirring
Of childhood's half-forgotten things?

Seest thou the dear old dwelling
With the woodbine round the door?
Brothers, soft! her breast is swelling
With the busy thoughts of yore;
Lowly sing ye, sing ye mildly,
Rouse her spirit not so wildly,
Lest she sleep not any more.
'T is the pleasant summertide,
Open stands the window wide —
Whose voices, Lady, art thou drinking?
Who sings that best belovèd tune
In a clear note, rising, sinking,
Like a thrush's song in June?
Whose laugh is that which rings so clear
And joyous in thine eager ear?

Lower, Brothers, yet more low
Weave the song in mazy twines;
She heareth now the west wind blow
At evening through the clump of pines;
O! mournful is their tune,
As of a crazèd thing

Who, to herself alone,
Is ever murmuring,
Through the night and through the day,
For something that hath passed away.
Often, Lady, hast thou listened,
Often have thy blue eyes glistened,
Where the summer evening breeze
Moaned sadly through those lonely trees,
Or with the fierce wind from the north
Wrung their mournful music forth.
Ever the river floweth
In an unbroken stream,
Ever the west wind bloweth,
Murmuring as he goeth,
And mingling with her dream;
Onward still the river sweepeth
With a sound of long-agone;
Lowly, Brothers, lo! she weepeth,
She is now no more alone;
Long-loved forms and long-loved faces
Round about her pillow throng,
Through her memory's desert places
Flow the waters of our song.
Lady! if thy life be holy
As when thou wert yet a child,
Though our song be melancholy,
It will stir no anguish wild;
For the soul that hath lived well,
For the soul that child-like is,
There is quiet in the spell
That brings back early memories.

SONG.

I.

LIFT up the curtains of thine eyes
   And let their light outshine!
Let me adore the mysteries
   Of those mild orbs of thine,
Which ever queenly calm do roll,
Attunèd to an ordered soul!

II.

Open thy lips yet once again
   And, while my soul doth hush
With awe, pour forth that holy strain
   Which seemeth me to gush,
A fount of music, running o'er
From thy deep spirit's inmost core!

III.

The melody that dwells in thee
   Begets in me as well
A spiritual harmony,
   A mild and blessèd spell;
Far, far above earth's atmosphere
I rise, whene'er thy voice I hear.

THE DEPARTED.

Not they alone are the departed,
Who have laid them down to sleep
In the grave narrow and lonely,
Not for them only do I vigils keep,
Not for them only am I heavy-hearted,
Not for them only!

Many, many, there are many
Who no more are with me here,
As cherished, as beloved as any
Whom I have seen upon the bier.
I weep to think of those old faces,
To see them in their grief or mirth;
I weep — for there are empty places
Around my heart's once crowded hearth;
The cold ground doth not cover them,
The grass hath not grown over them,
Yet are they gone from me on earth; —
O! how more bitter is this weeping,
Than for those lost ones who are sleeping
Where sun will shine and flowers blow,
Where gentle winds will whisper low,
And the stars have them in their keeping!
Wherefore from me who loved you so,
O! wherefore did ye go?
I have shed full many a tear,
I have wrestled oft in prayer —

But ye do not come again;
How could anything so dear,
How could anything so fair,
Vanish like the summer rain?
No, no, it cannot be,
But ye are still with me!

And yet, O! where art thou,
Childhood, with sunny brow
And floating hair?
Where art thou hiding now?
I have sought thee everywhere,
All among the shrubs and flowers
Of those garden-walks of ours —
Thou art not there!
When the shadow of Night's wings
Hath darkened all the Earth,
I listen to thy gambolings
Beside the cheerful hearth —
Thou art not there!
I listen to the far-off bell,
I murmur o'er the little songs
Which thou didst love so well,
Pleasant memories come in throngs
And mine eyes are blurred with tears,
But no glimpse of thee appears:
Lonely am I in the Winter, lonely in the Spring,
Summer and Harvest bring no trace of thee —
Oh! whither, whither art thou wandering,
Thou who didst once so cleave to me?

And Love is gone; —
I have seen him come,
I have seen him, too, depart,
Leaving desolate his home,
His bright home in my heart.
I am alone!
Cold, cold is his hearth-stone,
Wide open stands the door;
The frolic and the gentle one
Shall I see no more, no more?
At the fount the bowl is broken,
I shall drink it not again,
All my longing prayers are spoken,
And felt, ah, woe is me, in vain!
Oh, childish hopes and childish fancies,
Whither have ye fled away?
I long for you in mournful trances,
I long for you by night and day;
Beautiful thoughts that once were mine,
Might I but win you back once more,
Might ye about my being twine
And cluster as ye did of yore!
O! do not let me pray in vain —
How good and happy I should be,
How free from every shade of pain,
If ye would come again to me!
O, come again! come, come again!
Hath the sun forgot its brightness,
Have the stars forgot to shine,
That they bring not their wonted lightness
To this weary heart of mine?

'T is not the sun that shone on thee,
Happy childhood, long ago —
Not the same stars silently
Looking on the same bright snow —
Not the same that Love and I
Together watched in days gone by!
No, not the same, alas for me!

Would God that those who early went
To the house dark and low,
For whom our mourning heads were bent,
For whom our steps were slow;
O would that these alone had left us,
That Fate of these alone had reft us,
Would God indeed that it were so!
Many leaves too soon must wither,
Many flowers too soon must die,
Many bright ones wandering hither,
We know not whence, we know not why,
Like the leaves and like the flowers,
Vanish, ere the summer hours,
That brought them to us, have gone by.

O for the hopes and for the feelings,
Childhood, that I shared with thee —
The high resolves, the bright revealings
Of the soul's might, which thou gav'st me,
Gentle Love, woe worth the day,
Woe worth the hour when thou wert born,
Woe worth the day thou fled'st away —
A shade across the wind-waved corn —
A dewdrop falling from the leaves

Chance-shaken in a summer's morn!
Woe, woe is me! my sick heart grieves,
Companionless and anguish-worn!
I know it well, our manly years
Must be baptized in bitter tears;
Full many fountains must run dry
That youth has dreamed for long hours by,
Choked by convention's siroc blast
Or drifting sands of many cares;
Slowly they leave us all at last,
And cease their flowing unawares.

THE BOBOLINK.

ANACREON of the meadow,
Drunk with the joy of spring!
Beneath the tall pine's voiceful shadow
I lie and drink thy jargoning;
My soul is full with melodies,
One drop would overflow it,
And send the tears into mine eyes —
But what carest thou to know it?
Thy heart is free as mountain air,
And of thy lays thou hast no care,
Scattering them gayly everywhere,
Happy, unconscious poet!

Upon a tuft of meadow grass,
While thy loved-one tends the nest,
Thou swayest as the breezes pass,

The Bobolink.

Unburdening thine o'erfull breast
Of the crowded songs that fill it,
Just as joy may choose to will it.
Lord of thy love and liberty,
The blithest bird of merry May,
Thou turnest thy bright eyes on me,
That say as plain as eye can say —
" Here sit we, here in the summer weather,
I and my modest mate together ;
Whatever your wise thoughts may be,
Under that gloomy old pine-tree,
We do not value them a feather."

Now, leaving earth and me behind,
Thou beatest up against the wind,
Or, floating slowly down before it,
Above thy grass-hid nest thou flutterest
And thy bridal love-song utterest,
Raining showers of music o'er it,
Weary never, still thou trillest,
Spring-gladsome lays,
As of moss-rimmed water-brooks
Murmuring through pebbly nooks
In quiet summer days.
My heart with happiness thou fillest,
I seem again to be a boy
Watching thee, gay, blithesome lover,
O'er the bending grass-tops hover,
Quivering thy wings for joy.
There 's something in the apple-blossom,
The greening grass and bobolink's song,

That wakes again within my bosom
Feelings which have slumbered long.
As long, long years ago I wandered,
I seem to wander even yet,
The hours the idle school-boy squandered,
The man would die ere he'd forget.
O hours that frosty eld deemed wasted,
Nodding his gray head toward my books,
I dearer prize the lore I tasted
With you, among the trees and brooks,
Than all that I have gained since then
From learnèd books or study-withered men
Nature, thy soul was one with mine,
And, as a sister by a younger brother
Is loved, each flowing to the other,
Such love for me was thine.
Or wert thou not more like a loving mother
With sympathy and loving power to heal,
Against whose heart my throbbing head I 'd lay
And moan my childish sorrows all away,
Till calm and holiness would o'er me steal?
Was not the golden sunset a dear friend?
Found I no kindness in the silent moon,
And the green trees, whose tops did sway and bend,
Low singing evermore their pleasant tune?
Felt I no heart in dim and solemn woods –
No loved-one's voice in lonely solitudes?
Yes, yes! unhoodwinked then my spirit's eyes,
Blind leaders had not *taught me* to be wise.

  Dear hours! which now again I over-live,
Hearing and seeing with the ears and eyes

Of childhood, ye were bees, that to the hive
Of my young heart came laden with rich prize,
Gathered in fields and woods and sunny dells, to be
My spirit's food in days more wintery.
Yea, yet again ye come! ye come!
And, like a child once more at home
After long sojourning in alien climes,
I lie upon my mother's breast,
Feeling the blessedness of rest,
And dwelling in the light of other times.

O ye whose living is not *Life*,
Whose dying is but death,
Song, empty toil and petty strife,
Rounded with loss of breath!
Go, look on Nature's countenance,
Drink in the blessing of her glance;
Look on the sunset, hear the wind,
The cataract, the awful thunder;
Go, worship by the sea;
Then, and then only, shall ye find,
With ever-growing wonder,
Man is not all in all to ye;
Go with a meek and humble soul,
Then shall the scales of self unroll
From off your eyes — the weary packs
Drop from your heavy-laden backs;
And ye shall see,
With reverent and hopeful eyes,
Glowing with new-born energies,
How great a thing it is to BE!

FORGETFULNESS.

THERE 's a haven of sure rest
　From the loud world's bewildering stress:
As a bird dreaming on her nest,
As dew hid in a rose's breast,
As Hesper in the glowing West;
　　So the heart sleeps
　　In thy calm deeps,
　Serene Forgetfulness!

No sorrow in that place may be,
　The noise of life grows less and less:
As moss far down within the sea,
As, in white lily caves, a bee,
As life in a hazy reverie;
　　So the heart's wave
　　In thy dim cave,
　Hushes, Forgetfulness!

Duty and care fade far away;
　What toil may be we cannot guess:
As a ship anchored in the bay,
As a cloud at summer-noon astray,
As water-blooms in a breezeless day;
　　So, 'neath thine eyes,
　　The full heart lies,
　And dreams, Forgetfulness!

SONG.

I.

WHAT reck I of the stars, when I
   May gaze into thine eyes,
O'er which the brown hair flowingly
   Is parted maidenwise
From thy pale forehead, calm and bright,
Over thy cheeks so rosy white?

II.

What care I for the red moon-rise?
   Far liefer would I sit
And watch the joy within thine eyes
   Gush up at sight of it;
Thyself my queenly moon shall be,
Ruling my heart's deep tides for me!

III.

What heed I if the sky be blue?
   So are thy holy eyes,
And bright with shadows ever new
   Of changeful sympathies,
Which in thy soul's unruffled deep
Rest evermore, but never sleep.

THE POET.

He who hath felt Life's mystery
  Press on him like thick night,
Whose soul hath known no history
  But struggling after light; —
He who hath seen dim shapes arise
  In the soundless depths of soul,
Which gaze on him with meaning eyes
  Full of the mighty whole,
Yet will no word of healing speak,
  Although he pray night-long,
"O, help me, save me! I am weak,
  And ye are wondrous strong!" —
Who, in the midnight dark and deep,
  Hath felt a voice of might
Come echoing through the halls of sleep
  From the lone heart of Night,
And, starting from his restless bed,
  Hath watched and wept to know
What meant that oracle of dread
  That stirred his being so;
He who hath felt how strong and great
  This Godlike soul of man,
And looked full in the eyes of Fate,
  Since Life and Thought began;
The armor of whose moveless trust
  Knoweth no spot of weakness,
Who hath trod fear into the dust
  Beneath the feet of meekness; —
He who hath calmly borne his cross,
  Knowing himself the king

Of time, nor counted it a loss
　　To learn by suffering ; —
And who hath worshipped woman still
　　With a pure soul and lowly,
Nor ever hath in deed or will
　　Profaned her temple holy —
He is the Poet, him unto
　　The gift of song is given,
Whose life is lofty, strong, and true,
　　Who never fell from Heaven ;
He is the Poet, from his lips
　　To live forevermore,
Majestical as full-sailed ships,
　　The words of Wisdom pour.

FLOWERS.

" Hail be thou, holie hearbe,
　　Growing on the ground,
All in the mount Calvary
　　First wert thou found ;
Thou art good for manie a sore,
　　Thou healest manie a wound,
In the name of sweete Jesus
　　I take thee from the ground."
　　　　　　— *Ancient Charm-verse*

I.

When, from a pleasant ramble, home
Fresh-stored with quiet thoughts, I come,
I pluck some wayside flower
And press it in the choicest nook

Of a much-loved and oft-read book
And, when upon its leaves I look
In a less happy hour,
Dear memory bears me far away
Unto her fairy bower,
And on her breast my head I lay,
While, in a motherly, sweet strain,
She sings me gently back again
To by-gone feelings, until they
Seem children born of yesterday.

II.

Yes, many a story of past hours
I read in these dear withered flowers,
And once again I seem to be
Lying beneath the old oak-tree,
And looking up into the sky,
Through thick leaves rifted fitfully,
Lulled by the rustling of the vine,
Or the faint low of far-off kine;
And once again I seem
To watch the whirling bubbles flee,
Through shade and gleam alternately,
Down the vine-bowered stream;
Or 'neath the odorous linden-trees,
When summer twilight lingers long,
To hear the flowing of the breeze
And unseen insects' slumberous song,
That mingle into one and seem
Like dim murmurs of a dream;

Fair faces, too, I seem to see,
Smiling from pleasant eyes at me,
And voices sweet I hear,
That, like remembered melody,
Flow through my spirit's ear.

III.

A poem every flower is,
And every leaf a line,
And with delicious memories
They fill this heart of mine:
No living blossoms are so clear
As these dead relics treasured here;
One tells of love, of friendship one,
Love's quiet after-sunset time,
When the all-dazzling light is gone,
And, with the soul's low vesper-chime,
O'er half its heaven doth out-flow
A holy calm and steady glow.
Some are gay feast-song, some are dirges,
In some a joy with sorrow merges;
One sings the shadowed woods, and one the
   roar
Of ocean's everlasting surges,
Tumbling upon the beach's hard-beat floor,
Or sliding backward from the shore
To meet the landward waves and slowly
   plunge once more.
O flowers of grace, I bless ye all
By the dear faces ye recall!

IV.

Upon the banks of Life's deep streams
Full many a flower groweth,
Which with a wondrous fragrance teems,
And in the silent water gleams,
And trembles as the water floweth;
Many a one the wave upteareth,
Washing ever the roots away,
And far upon its bosom beareth,
To bloom no more in Youth's glad May.
As farther on the river runs,
Flowing more deep and strong,
Only a few pale, scattered ones
Are seen the dreary banks along;
And where those flowers do not grow,
The river floweth dark and chill,
Its voice is sad, and with its flow
Mingles ever a sense of ill;
Then, Poet, thou who gather dost
Of Life's best flowers the brightest,
O, take good heed they be not lost
While with the angry flood thou fightest!

V.

In the cool grottos of the soul,
Whence flows thought's crystal river,
Whence songs of joy forever roll
To Him who is the Giver —
There store thou them, where fresh and green

Their leaves and blossoms may be seen,
A spring of joy that faileth never;
There store thou them, and they shall be
A blessing and a peace to thee,
And in their youth and purity
Thou shalt be young forever!
Then, with their fragrance rich and rare,
Thy living shall be rife,
Strength shall be thine thy cross to bear,
And they shall be a chaplet fair,
Breathing a pure and holy air,
To crown thy holy life.

VI.

O Poet! above all men blest,
Take heed that thus thou store them;
Love, Hope, and Faith shall ever rest,
Sweet birds (upon how sweet a nest!)
Watchfully brooding o'er them.
And from those flowers of Paradise
Scatter thou many a blessèd seed,
Wherefrom an offspring may arise
To cheer the hearts and light the eyes
Of after-voyagers in their need.
They shall not fall on stony ground,
But, yielding all their hundred-fold,
Shall shed a peacefulness around,
Whose strengthening joy may not be told,
So shall thy name be blest of all,
And thy remembrance never die;

For of that seed shall surely fall
In the fair garden of Eternity.
Exult then in the nobleness
Of this thy work so holy,
Yet be not thou one jot the less
Humble and meek and lowly,
But let thine exultation be
The reverence of a bended knee;
And by thy life a poem write,
Built strongly day by day—
And on the rock of Truth and Right
Its deep foundations lay.

VII.

It is thy DUTY! Guard it well!
For unto thee hath much been given,
And thou canst make this life a Hell,
Or Jacob's-ladder up to Heaven.
Let not thy baptism in Life's wave
Make thee like him whom Homer sings—
A sleeper in a living grave,
Callous and hard to outward things;
But open all thy soul and sense
To every blessèd influence
That from the heart of Nature springs:
Then shall thy Life-flowers be to thee,
When thy best years are told,
As much as these have been to me—
Yea, more, a thousand-fold!

THE LOVER.

I.

Go from the world from East to West,
Search every land beneath the sky,
You cannot find a man so blest,
A king so powerful as I,
Though you should seek eternally.

II.

For I a gentle lover be,
Sitting at my loved-one's side ;
She giveth her whole soul to me
Without a wish or thought of pride,
And she shall be my cherished bride.

III.

No show of gaudiness hath she,
She doth not flash with jewels rare ;
In beautiful simplicity
She weareth leafy garlands fair,
Or modest flowers in her hair.

IV.

Sometimes she dons a robe of green,
Sometimes a robe of snowy white,
But, in whatever garb she's seen,
It seems most beautiful and right,
And is the loveliest to my sight.

v.

Not I her lover am alone,
Yet unto all she doth suffice,
None jealous is, and every one
Reads love and truth within her eyes,
And deemeth her his own dear prize.

vi.

And so thou art, Eternal Nature!
Yes, bride of Heaven, so thou art;
Thou wholly lovest every creature,
Giving to each no stinted part,
But filling every peaceful heart.

TO E. W. G.

"DEAR Child! dear happy Girl! if thou appear
Heedless — untouched with awe or serious thought,
Thy nature is not therefore less divine:
Thou liest in Abraham's bosom all the year;
And worship'st at the Temple's inner shrine,
God being with thee when we know it not."

— Wordsworth.

As through a strip of sunny light
A white dove flashes swiftly on,
So suddenly before my sight
Thou gleamed'st a moment and wert gone;
And yet I long shall bear in mind
The pleasant thoughts thou left'st behind.

Thou madest me happy with thine eyes,
And happy with thine open smile,
And, as I write, sweet memories
Come thronging round me all the while;
Thou madest me happy with thine eyes —
And gentle feelings long forgot
Looked up and oped their eyes,
Like violets when they see a spot
Of summer in the skies.

Around thy playful lips did glitter
Heat-lightnings of a girlish scorn;
Harmless they were, for nothing bitter
In thy dear heart was ever born —
That merry heart that could not lie
Within its warm nest quietly,
But ever from each full, dark eye
Was looking kindly night and morn.

There was an archness in thine eyes,
Born of the gentlest mockeries,
And thy light laughter rang as clear
As water-drops I loved to hear
In days of boyhood, as they fell
Tinkling far down the dim, still well;
And with its sound come back once more
The feelings of my early years,
And half aloud I murmured o'er —
" Sure I have heard that sound before,
It is so pleasant in mine ears."

Whenever thou didst look on me
I thought of merry birds,
And something of spring's melody
Came to me in thy words;
Thy thoughts did dance and bound along
Like happy children in their play,
Whose hearts run over into song
For gladness of the summer's day;
And mine grew dizzy with the sight,
Still feeling lighter and more light,
Till, joining hands, they whirled away,
As blithe and merrily as they.

I bound a larch-twig round with flowers,
Which thou didst twine among thy hair,
And gladsome were the few, short hours
When I was with thee there;
So now that thou art far away,
Safe-nestled in thy warmer clime,
In memory of a happier day
I twine this simple wreath of rhyme.

Dost mind how she, whom thou dost love
More than in light words may be said,
A coronal of amaranth wove
About thy duly-sobered head,
Which kept itself a moment still
That she might have her gentle will?
Thy childlike grace and purity
O keep forevermore,
And as thou art, still strive to be,
That on the farther shore

Of Time's dark waters ye may meet,
And she may twine around thy brow
A wreath of those bright flowers that grow
Where blessèd angels set their feet!

ISABEL.

As the leaf upon the tree,
Fluttering, gleaming constantly,
Such a lightsome thing was she,
My gay and gentle Isabel!
Her heart was fed with love-springs sweet,
And in her face you'd see it beat
To hear the sound of welcome feet —
And were not mine so, Isabel?

She knew it not, but she was fair,
And like a moonbeam was her hair,
That falls where flowing ripples are
In summer evenings, Isabel!
Her heart and tongue were scarce apart,
Unwittingly her lips would part,
And love came gushing from her heart,
The woman's heart of Isabel.

So pure her flesh-garb, and like dew,
That in her features glimmered through
Each working of her spirit true,
In wondrous beauty, Isabel!

A sunbeam struggling through thick leaves,
A reaper's song mid yellow sheaves,
Less gladsome were ; — my spirit grieves
To think of thee, mild Isabel!

I know not when I loved thee first ;
Not loving, I had been accurst,
Yet, having loved, my heart will burst,
Longing for thee, dear Isabel !
With silent tears my cheeks are wet,
I would be calm, I would forget,
But thy blue eyes gaze on me yet,
When stars have risen, Isabel.

The winds mourn for thee, Isabel,
The flowers expect thee in the dell,
Thy gentle spirit loved them well,
And I for thy sake, Isabel !
The sunsets seem less lovely now
Than when, leaf checkered, on thy brow
They fell as lovingly as thou
Lingered'st till moon-rise, Isabel !

At dead of night I seem to see
Thy fair, pale features constantly
Upturned in silent prayer for me,
O'er moveless clasped hands, Isabel !
I call thee, thou dost not reply ;
The stars gleam coldly on thine eye,
As like a dream thou flittest by,
And leav'st me weeping, Isabel !

MUSIC.

I.

I SEEM to lie with drooping eyes,
  Dreaming sweet dreams,
Half longings and half memories,
  In woods where streams
With trembling shades and whirling gleams,
  Many and bright,
  In song and light,
  Are ever, ever flowing;
While the wind, if we list to the rustling grass,
Which numbers his footsteps as they pass,
  Seems scarcely to be blowing;
And the far-heard voice of Spring,
From sunny slopes comes wandering,
Calling the violets from the sleep,
That bound them under the snow-drifts deep,
To open their childlike, asking eyes
On the new summer's paradise,
And mingled with the gurgling waters —
  As the dreamy witchery
Of Acheloüs' silver-voiced daughters
  Rose and fell with the heaving sea,
  Whose great heart swelled with ecstasy —
The song of many a floating bird,
  Winding through the rifted trees,
Is dreamily half-heard —
  A sister stream of melodies
Rippled by the flutterings
Of rapture-quivered wings.

II.

And now beside a cataract
I lie, and through my soul,
From over me and under,
The never-ceasing thunder
Arousingly doth roll;
Through the darkness all compact,
Through the trackless sea of gloom,
Sad and deep I hear it boom;
At intervals the cloud is cracked
And a livid flash doth hiss
   Downward from its floating home,
Lighting up the precipice
   And the never-resting foam
With a dim and ghastly glare,
Which, for a heart-beat, in the air,
   Shows the sweeping shrouds
   Of the midnight clouds
And their wildly-scattered hair

III.

Now listening to a woman's tone,
In a wood I sit alone —
Alone because our souls are one; —
All around my heart it flows,
Lulling me in deep repose;
I fear to speak, I fear to move,

Lest I should break the spell I love —
Low and gentle, calm and clear,
Into my inmost soul it goes,
   As if my brother dear,
   Who is no longer here,
   Had bended from the sky
   And murmured in my ear
A strain of that high harmony,
   Which they may sing alone
   Who worship round the throne.

IV.

Now in a fairy boat,
   On the bright waves of song,
Full merrily I float,
   Merrily float along;
   My helm is veered, I care not how,
   My white sail bellies over me,
And bright as gold the ripples be
That plash beneath the bow;
   Before, behind,
   They feel the wind,
   And they are dancing joyously —
While, faintly heard, along the far-off shore
The surf goes plunging with a lingering roar;
Or anchored in a shadowy cove,
   Entranced with harmonies,
   Slowly I sink and rise
As the slow waves of music move.

v.

Now softly dashing,
Bubbling, plashing,
Mazy, dreamy,
Faint and streamy,
Ripples into ripples melt,
Not so strongly heard as felt;
Now rapid and quick,
While the heart beats thick,
The music's silver wavelets crowd,
Distinct and clear, but never loud;
And now all solemnly and slow,
In mild, deep tones they warble low,
Like the glad song of angels, when
They sang good will and peace to men;
Now faintly heard and far,
  As if the spirit's ears
Had caught the anthem of a star
  Chanting with his brother-spheres
In the midnight dark and deep,
When the body is asleep
And wondrous shadows pour in streams
From the twofold gate of dreams;
Now onward roll the billows, swelling
With a tempest-sound of might,
As of voices doom foretelling
  To the silent ear of Night;
And now a mingled ecstasy
  Of all sweet sounds it is; —
  O! who may tell the agony
    Of rapture such as this?

VI.

I have drunk of the drink of immortals,
   I have drunk of the life-giving wine,
And now I may pass the bright portals
   That open into a realm divine!
I have drunk it through mine ears
   In the ecstasy of song,
When mine eyes would fill with tears
   That its life were not more long;
I have drunk it through mine eyes
   In beauty's every shape,
And now around my soul it lies,
   No juice of earthly grape!
Wings! wings are given to me;
   I can flutter, I can rise,
Like a new life gushing through me;
   Sweep the heavenly harmonies!

SONG.

O! I MUST look on that sweet face once more before
   I die;
God grant that it may lighten up with joy when I
   draw nigh;
God grant that she may look on me as kindly as she
   seems
In the long night, the restless night, i' the sunny land
   of dreams!

I hoped, I thought, she loved me once, and yet, I
  know not why,
There is a coldness in her speech, and a coldness in
  her eye.
Something that in another's look would not seem cold
  to me,
And yet like ice I feel it chill the heart of memory.

She does not come to greet me so frankly as she did,
And in her utmost openness I feel there 's something
  hid;
She almost seems to shun me, as if she thought
  that I
Might win her gentle heart again to feelings long
  gone by.

I sought the first spring-buds for her, the fairest and
  the best,
And she wore them for their loveliness upon her
  spotless breast,
The blood-root and the violet, the frail anemone,
She wore them, and alas! I deemed it was for love
  of me!

As flowers in a darksome place stretch forward to the
  light,
So to the memory of her I turn by day and night;
As flowers in a darksome place grow thin and pale
  and wan,
So is it with my darkened heart, now that her light
  is gone.

The thousand little things that love doth treasure up
    for aye,
And brood upon with moistened eyes when she that 's
    loved 's away,
The word, the look, the smile, the blush, the ribbon
    that she wore,
Each day they grow more dear to me, and pain me
    more and more.

My face I cover with my hands, and bitterly I weep,
That the quick-gathering sands of life should choke
    a love so deep,
And that the stream, so pure and bright, must turn
    it from its track,
Or to the heart-springs, whence it rose, roll its full
    waters back!

As calm as doth the lily float close by the lakelet's
    brim,
So calm and spotless, down time's stream, her peace-
    ful days did swim,
And I had longed, and dreamed, and prayed, that
    closely by her side,
Down to a haven still and sure, my happy life might
    glide.

But now, alas! those golden days of youth and hope
    are o'er,
And I must dream those dreams of joy, those guilt-
    less dreams no more;

Yet there is something in my heart that whispers
   ceaselessly,
"Would God that I might see that face once more
   before I die!"

———

IANTHE.

I.

THERE is a light within her eyes,
Like gleams of wandering fire-flies;
From light to shade it leaps and moves
Whenever in her soul arise
The holy shapes of things she loves;
Fitful it shines and changes ever,
Like star-lit ripples on a river,
Or summer sunshine on the eaves
Of silver-trembling poplar leaves,
Where the lingering dew-drops quiver.
I may not tell the blessedness
Her mild eyes send to mine,
The sunset-tinted haziness
Of their mysterious shine,
The dim and holy mournfulnes
Of their mellow light divine;
The shadow of the lashes lie
Over them so lovingly,
That they seem to melt away
In a doubtful twilight-gray,

While I watch the stars arise
In the evening of her eyes.
I love it, yet I almost dread
To think what it foreshadoweth;
And, when I muse how I have read
That such strange light betokened death —
Instead of fire-fly gleams, I see
Wild corpse-lights gliding waveringly.

II.

With wayward thoughts her eyes are bright,
Like shiftings of the northern-light,
Hither, thither, swiftly glance they,
In a mazy twining dance they,
Like ripply lights the sunshine weaves,
Thrown backward from a shaken nook,
Below some tumbling water-brook,
On the o'erarching platan-leaves,
All through her glowing face they flit,
And rest in their deep dwelling-place,
Those fathomless blue eyes of hers,
Till, from her burning soul re-lit,
While her upheaving bosom stirs,
They stream again across her face
And with such hope and glory fill it,
Death could not have the heart to chill it.
Yet when their wild light fades again,
I feel a sudden sense of pain,

As if, while yet her eyes were gleaming,
And like a shower of sun-lit rain
Bright fancies from her face were streaming,
Her trembling soul might flit away
As swift and suddenly as they.

III.

A wild, inspirèd earnestness
    Her inmost being fills,
And eager self-forgetfulness,
    That speaks not what it wills,
But what unto her soul is given,
A living oracle from Heaven,
Which scarcely in her breast is born
When on her trembling lips it thrills,
And, like a burst of golden skies
Through storm-clouds on a sudden torn,
Like a glory of the morn,
Beams marvellously from her eyes.
And then, like a Spring-swollen river,
Roll the deep waves of her full-hearted thought
    Crested with sun-lit spray,
    Her wild lips curve and quiver,
And my rapt soul, on the strong tide upcaught,
    Unwittingly is borne away,
    Lulled by a dreamful music ever,
    Far — through the solemn twilight-gray
    Of hoary woods — through valleys green
    Which the trailing vine embowers,
And where the purple-clustered grapes are seen

Deep-glowing through rich clumps of waving flow-
    ers —
    Now over foaming rapids swept
    And with maddening rapture shook —
Now gliding where the water-plants have slept
    For ages in a moss-rimmed nook —
    Enwoven by a wild-eyed band
        Of earth-forgetting dreams,
    I float to a delicious land
    By a sunset heaven spanned,
        And musical with streams ; —
    Around, the calm, majestic forms
And god-like eyes of early Greece I see,
    Or listen, till my spirit warms,
    To songs of courtly chivalry,
Or weep, unmindful if my tears be seen,
For the meek, suffering love of poor Undine.

IV.

    Her thoughts are never memories,
    But ever changeful, ever new,
    Fresh and beautiful as dew
    That in a dell at noontide lies,
    Or, at the close of summer day,
    The pleasant breath of new-mown hay :
    Swiftly they come and pass
    As golden birds across the sun,
    As light-gleams on tall meadow-grass
    Which the wind just breathes upon.
    And when she speaks, her eyes I see

Down-gushing through their silken lattices,
 Like stars that quiver tremblingly
 Through leafy branches of the trees,
And her pale cheeks do flush and glow
 With speaking flashes bright and rare
As crimson North-lights on new-fallen snow,
 From out the veiling of her hair —
Her careless hair that scatters down
 On either side her eyes,
A waterfall leaf-tinged with brown
 And lit with the sunrise.

v.

 When first I saw her, not of earth,
But heavenly both in grief and mirth,
I thought her; she did seem
As fair and full of mystery,
As bodiless, as forms we see
In the rememberings of a dream;
A moon-lit mist, a strange, dim light,
Circled her spirit from my sight; —
Each day more beautiful she grew,
 More earthly every day,
Yet that mysterious, moony hue
 Faded not all away;
She has a sister's sympathy
With all the wanderers of the sky,
But most I 've seen her bosom stir
 When moonlight round her fell,
For the mild moon it loveth her,

She loveth it as well,
And of their love perchance this grace
Was born into her wondrous face.
I cannot tell how it may be,
For both, methinks, can scarce be true,
Still, as she earthly grew to me,
She grew more heavenly too;
    She seems one born in Heaven
        With earthly feelings,
    For, while unto her soul are given
    More pure revealings
    Of holiest love and truth,
Yet is the mildness of her eyes
Made up of quickest sympathies,
    Of kindliness and ruth;
So, though some shade of awe doth stir
Our souls for one so far above us,
We feel secure that she will love us,
And cannot keep from loving her.
She is a poem, which to me
In speech and look is written bright,
And to her life's rich harmony
Doth ever sing itself aright;
Dear, glorious creature!
With eyes so dewy bright,
    And tenderest feeling
    Itself revealing
In every look and feature,
Welcome as a homestead light
To one long-wandering in a clouded night;
    O lovelier for her woman's weakness,

Which yet is strongly mailed
In armor of courageous meekness
And faith that never failed!

VI.

Early and late, at her soul's gate,
Sits Chastity in warderwise,
No thoughts unchallenged, small or great,
Go thence into her eyes;
Nor may a low, unworthy thought
Beyond that virgin warder win,
Nor one, whose password is not " ought,"
May go without or enter in.
I call her, seeing those pure eyes,
The Eve of a new Paradise,
Which she by gentle word and deed,
And look no less, doth still create
About her, for her great thoughts breed
A calm that lifts us from our fallen state,
And makes us while with her both good and great —
Nor is their memory wanting in our need:
With stronger loving, every hour,
Turneth my heart to this frail flower,
Which, thoughtless of the world, hath grown
To beauty and meek gentleness,
Here in a fair world of its own —
By woman's instinct trained alone —
A lily fair which God did bless,
And which from Nature's heart did draw
Love, wisdom, peace, and Heaven's perfect law.

LOVE'S ALTAR.

I.

I BUILT an altar in my soul,
I builded it to one alone ;
And ever silently I stole,
In happy days of long-agone,
To make rich offerings to that ONE.

II.

'T was garlanded with purest thought,
And crowned with fancy's flowers bright,
With choicest gems 't was all inwrought
Of truth and feeling ; in my sight
It seemed a spot of cloudless light.

III.

Yet when I made my offering there,
Like Cain's, the incense would not rise ;
Back on my heart down-sank the prayer,
And altar-stone and sacrifice
Grew hateful in my tear-dimmed eyes.

IV.

O'er-grown with age's mosses green,
The little altar firmly stands;
It is not, as it once hath been,
A selfish shrine; — these time-taught hands
Bring incense now from many lands.

V.

Knowledge doth only widen love;
The stream, that lone and narrow rose,
Doth, deepening ever, onward move,
And with an even current flows
Calmer and calmer to the close.

VI.

The love, that in those early days
Girt round my spirit like a wall,
Hath faded like a morning haze,
And flames, unpent by self's mean thrall,
Rise clearly to the perfect ALL.

MY LOVE.

I.

NOT as all other women are
Is she that to my soul is dear;
Her glorious fancies come from far
Beneath the silver evening-star,
And yet her heart is ever near.

II.

Great feelings hath she of her own
Which lesser souls may never know;
God giveth them to her alone,
And sweet they are as any tone
Wherewith the wind may choose to blow.

III.

Yet in herself she dwelleth not,
Although no home were half so fair;
No simplest duty is forgot,
Life hath no dim and lowly spot
That doth not in her sunshine share.

IV.

She doeth little kindnesses,
Which most leave undone, or despise,
For naught that sets one heart at ease,
And giveth happiness or peace,
Is low-esteemèd in her eyes.

V.

She hath no scorn of common things
And, though she seem of other birth,
Round us her heart entwines and clings,
And patiently she folds her wings
To tread the humble paths of earth.

VI.

Blessing she is : God made her so,
And deeds of week-day holiness
Fall from her noiseless as the snow,
Nor hath she ever chanced to know
That aught were easier than to bless.

VII.

She is most fair, and thereunto
Her life doth rightly harmonize ;
Feeling or thought that was not true
Ne'er made less beautiful the blue
Unclouded heaven of her eyes.

VIII.

On Nature she doth muse and brood
With such a still and love-clear eye —
She is so gentle and so good —
The very flowers in the wood
Do bless her with their sympathy.

IX.

She is a woman: one in whom
The spring-time of her childish years
Hath never lost its fresh perfume,
Though knowing well that life hath room
For many blights and many tears.

X.

And youth in her a home will find,
Where he may dwell eternally;
Her soul is not of that weak kind
Which better love the life behind
Than that which is, or is to be.

XI.

I love her with a love as still
As a broad river's peaceful might,
Which, by high tower and lowly mill,
Goes wandering at its own will,
And yet doth ever flow aright.

XII.

And, on its full, deep breast serene,
Like quiet isles my duties lie;
It flows around them and between,
And makes them fresh and fair and green,
Sweet homes wherein to live and die.

WITH A PRESSED FLOWER.

THIS little flower from afar
Hath come from other lands to thine;
For, once, its white and drooping star
Could see its shadow in the Rhine.

Perchance some fair-haired German maid
Hath plucked one from the self-same stalk,
And numbered over, half afraid,
Its petals in her evening walk.

"He loves me, loves me not," she cries;
"He loves me more than earth or Heaven,"
And then glad tears have filled her eyes
To find the number was uneven.

So, Love, my heart doth wander forth
To farthest lands beyond the sea,
And search the fairest spots of earth
To find sweet flowers of thought for thee.

A type this tiny blossom is
Of what my heart doth every day,
Seeking for pleasant fantasies
To brood upon when thou 'rt away.

And thou must count its petals well,
Because it is a gift from me;
And the last one of all shall tell
Something I 've often told to thee.

But here at home, where we were born,
Thou wilt find flowers just as true,
Down bending every summer morn
With freshness of New England dew.

For Nature, ever right in love,
Hath given them the same sweet tongue,
Whether with German skies above,
Or here our granite rocks among.

IMPARTIALITY.

I.

I CANNOT say a scene is fair
Because it is beloved of thee,
But I shall love to linger there,
For sake of thy dear memory;
I would not be so coldly just
As to love only what I must.

II.

I cannot say a thought is good
Because thou foundest joy in it;
Each soul must choose its proper food
Which Nature hath decreed most fit;
But I shall ever deem it so
Because it made thy heart o'erflow.

III.

I love thee for that thou art fair;
And that thy spirit joys in aught
Createth a new beauty there,
With thine own dearest image fraught;
And love, for others' sake that springs,
Gives half their charm to lovely things.

BELLEROPHON.

DEDICATED TO MY FRIEND, JOHN F. HEATH.

I.

I FEEL the bandages unroll
That bound my inward seeing;
Freed are the bright wings of my soul,
Types of my godlike being;
High thoughts are swelling in my heart

And rushing through my brain;
May I never more lose part
In my soul's realm again!
All things fair, where'er they be,
In earth or air, in sky or sea,
I have loved them all, and taken
All within my throbbing breast;
No more my spirit can be shaken
From its calm and kingly rest!
Love hath shed its light around me,
Love hath pierced the shades that bound me;
Mine eyes are opened, I can see
The universe's mystery,
   The mighty heart and core
   Of After and Before
I see, and I am weak no more!

II.

Upward! upward evermore,
To Heaven's open gate I soar!
Little thoughts are far behind me,
Which, when custom weaves together,
All the nobler man can tether —
Cobwebs now no more can bind me!
Now fold thy wings a little while,
   My trancèd soul, and lie
At rest on this Calypso-isle
   That floats in mellow sky,
A thousand isles with gentle motion
Rock upon the sunset ocean;

A thousand isles of thousand hues,
How bright! how beautiful! how rare!
Into my spirit they infuse
A purer, a diviner air;
The earth is growing dimmer,
And now the last faint glimmer
  Hath faded from the hill;
But in my higher atmosphere
The sunlight streameth red and clear,
  Fringing the islets still;—
Love lifts us to the sunlight,
Though the whole world would be dark;
Love, wide Love, is the *one* light,
All else is but a fading spark;
Love is the nectar which doth fill
Our soul's cup even to overflowing,
And, warming heart, and thought, and will,
Doth lie within us mildly glowing,
From its own centre raying out
Beauty and Truth on all without.

III.

  Each on his golden throne,
Full royally, alone,
I see the stars above me,
With sceptre and with diadem;
Mildly they look down and love me,
For I have ever yet loved them;
I see their ever-sleepless eyes
Watching the growth of destinies;

Calm, sedate,
The eyes of Fate,
They wink not, nor do roll,
But search the depths of soul —
And in those mighty depths they see
The germs of all Futurity,
Waiting but the fitting time
To burst and ripen into prime,
As in the womb of mother Earth
The seeds of plants and forests lie
Age upon age and never die —
So in the souls of all men wait,
Undyingly the seeds of Fate;
Chance breaks the clod and forth they spring,
Filling blind men with wondering.
Eternal stars! with holy awe,
As if a present God I saw,
I look into those mighty eyes
And see great destinies arise,
As in those of mortal men
Feelings glow and fade again!
All things below, all things above,
Are open to the eyes of Love.

IV.

Of Knowledge Love is master-key,
Knowledge of Beauty; passing dear
Is each to each, and mutually
Each one doth make the other clear;

Beauty is Love, and what we love
Straightway is beautiful,
So is the circle round and full,
And so dear Love doth live and move
   And have his being,
Finding his proper food
   By sure inseeing,
In all things pure and good,
Which he at will doth cull,
Like a joyous butterfly
Hiving in the sunny bowers
Of the soul's fairest flowers,
Or, between the earth and sky,
Wandering at liberty
For happy, happy hours!

v.

   The thoughts of Love are Poesy,
As this fair earth and all we see
Are the thoughts of Deity —
And Love is ours by our birthright!
He hath cleared mine inward sight;
Glorious shapes with glorious eyes
Round about my spirit glance,
Shedding a mild and golden light
On the shadowy face of Night;
To unearthly melodies,
Hand in hand, they weave their dance,

While a deep, ambrosial lustre
   From their rounded limbs doth shine,
Through many a rich and golden cluster
   Of streaming hair divine.
In our gross and earthly hours
We cannot see the Love-given powers
Which ever round the soul await
   To do its sovereign will,
When, in its moments calm and still,
It re-assumes its royal state,
Nor longer sits with eyes downcast,
A beggar, dreaming of the past,
At its own palace-gate.

VI.

   I too am a Maker and a Poet;
Through my whole soul I feel it and know it;
My veins are fired with ecstasy!
   All-mother Earth
   Did ne'er give birth
To one who shall be matched with me;
The lustre of my coronal
Shall cast a dimness over all. —
Alas! alas! what have I spoken?
My strong, my eagle wings are broken,
And back again to earth I fall!

SOMETHING NATURAL.

I.

WHEN first I saw thy soul-deep eyes,
My heart yearned to thee instantly,
Strange longing in my soul did rise;
I cannot tell the reason why,
But I must love thee till I die.

II.

The sight of thee hath well-nigh grown
As needful to me as the light;
I am unrestful when alone,
And my heart doth not beat aright
Except it dwell within thy sight.

III.

And yet — and yet — O selfish love!
I am not happy even with thee;
I see thee in thy brightness move,
And cannot well contented be,
Save thou should'st shine alone for me.

IV.

We should love beauty even as flowers —
For all, 't is said, they bud and blow,
They are the world's as well as ours —
But thou — alas ! God made thee grow
So fair, I cannot love thee so !

THE SIRENS.

THE sea is lonely, the sea is dreary,
  The sea is restless and uneasy ;
Thou seekest quiet, thou art weary,
Wandering thou knowest not whither ; —
Our little isle is green and breezy,
Come and rest thee ! O come hither,
Come to this peaceful home of ours,
      Where evermore
The low west-wind creeps panting up the shore
  To be at rest among the flowers ;
Full of rest, the green moss lifts,
  As the dark waves of the sea
Draw in and out of rocky rifts,
  Calling solemnly to thee,
With voices deep and hollow —
      To the shore
  Follow ! O follow !
To be at rest for evermore !
      For evermore !

Look how the gray, old Ocean
From the depths of his heart rejoices,
Heaving with a gentle motion,
When he hears our restful voices;
List how he sings in an undertone,
Chiming with our melody;
And all sweet sounds of earth and air
Melt into one low voice alone,
That murmurs over the weary sea—
And seems to sing from everywhere—
"Here mayest thou harbor peacefully,
Here mayest thou rest from the aching oar;
  Turn thy curvèd prow ashore,
And in our green isle rest for evermore!
     For evermore!
And Echo half wakes in the wooded hill,
  And, to her heart so calm and deep,
  Murmurs over in her sleep,
Doubtfully pausing and murmuring still,
    "Evermore!"
    Thus, on Life's weary sea,
    Heareth the marinere
    Voices sweet, from far and near,
    Ever singing low and clear,
    Ever singing longingly.

  Is it not better here to be,
Than to be toiling late and soon?
In the dreary night to see
Nothing but the blood-red moon

Go up and down into the sea;
Or, in the loneliness of day,
  To see the still seals only,
Solemnly lift their faces gray,
  Making it yet more lonely?
Is it not better, than to hear
Only the sliding of the wave
Beneath the plank, and feel so near
A cold and lonely grave,
A restless grave, where thou shalt lie
Even in death unquietly?
Look down beneath thy wave-worn bark,
  Lean over the side and see
The leaden eye of the side-long shark
        Upturnèd patiently
  Ever waiting there for thee:
Look down and see those shapeless forms,
  Which ever keep their dreamless sleep
  Far down within the gloomy deep,
And only stir themselves in storms,
Rising like islands from beneath,
And snorting through the angry spray,
As the frail vessel perisheth
In the whirls of their unwieldly play;
        Look down! Look down!
Upon the seaweed, slimy and dark,
That waves its arms so lank and brown,
        Beckoning for thee!
Look down beneath thy wave-worn bark
  Into the cold depth of the sea!
        Look down! Look down!

Thus, on Life's lonely sea,
Heareth the marinere
Voices sad, from far and near,
Ever singing full of fear,
Ever singing drearfully.

Here all is pleasant as a dream;
The wind scarce shaketh down the dew,
The green grass floweth like a stream
Into the ocean's blue:
Listen! O listen!
Here is a gush of many streams,
A song of many birds,
And every wish and longing seems
Lulled to a numbered flow of words —
Listen! O listen!
Here ever hum the golden bees
Underneath full-blossomed trees,
At once with glowing fruit and flower crowned; —
The sand is so smooth, the yellow sand,
That thy keel will not grate, as it touches the land;
All around, with a slumberous sound,
The singing waves slide up the strand,
And there, where the smooth wet pebbles be,
The waters gurgle longingly,
As if they fain would seek the shore,
To be at rest from the ceaseless roar,
To be at rest for evermore —
For evermore.
Thus, on Life's gloomy sea,

Heareth the marinere
Voices sweet, far and near,
Ever singing in his ear,
Here is rest and peace for thee!"

NANTASKET, July, 1840.

A FEELING.

THE flowers and the grass to me
Are eloquent reproachfully;
For would they wave so pleasantly
Or look so fresh and fair,
If a man, cunning, hollow, mean,
Or one in anywise unclean,
Were looking on them there?

No; he hath grown so foolish-wise
He cannot see with childhood's eyes;
He hath forgot that purity
And lowliness which are the key
Of Nature's mysteries;
No; he hath wandered off so long
From his own place of birth,
That he hath lost his mother-tongue,
And, like one come from far-off lands,
Forgetting and forgot, he stands
Beside his mother's hearth.

THE BEGGAR.

A BEGGAR through the world am I,
From place to place I wander by; —
Fill up my pilgrim's scrip for me,
For Christ's sweet sake and charity!

A little of thy steadfastness,
Rounded with leafy gracefulness,
Old oak, give me —
That the world's blasts may round me blow,
And I yield gently to and fro,
While my stout-hearted trunk below
And firm-set roots unmovèd be.

Some of thy stern, unyielding might,
Enduring still through day and night
Rude tempest-shock and withering blight —
That I may keep at bay
The changeful April sky of chance
And the strong tide of circumstance —
Give me, old granite gray.

Some of thy mournfulness serene,
Some of thy never-dying green,
Put in this scrip of mine —
That grief may fall like snowflakes light,
And deck me in a robe of white,
Ready to be an angel bright —
O sweetly-mournful pine.

A little of thy merriment,
Of thy sparkling, light content,
Give me my cheerful brook —
That I may still be full of glee
And gladsomeness, where'er I be,
Though fickle fate hath prisoned me
In some neglected nook.

Ye have been very kind and good
To me, since I've been in the wood;
Ye have gone nigh to fill my heart;
But good-by, kind friends, every one,
I 've far to go ere set of sun;
Of all good things I would have part,
The day was high ere I could start,
And so my journey 's scarce begun.

Heaven help me! how could I forget
To beg of thee, dear violet!
Some of thy modesty,
That flowers here as well, unseen,
As if before the world thou 'dst been,
O give, to strengthen me.

SERENADE.

From the close-shut windows gleams no spark,
The night is chilly, the night is dark,
The poplars shiver, the pine-trees moan,
My hair by the autumn breeze is blown,
Under thy window I sing alone,
Alone, alone, ah woe! alone!

The darkness is pressing coldly around,
The windows shake with a lonely sound,
The stars are hid and the night is drear,
The heart of silence throbs in thine ear,
In thy chamber thou sittest alone,
Alone, alone, ah woe! alone!

The world is happy, the world is wide,
Kind hearts are beating on every side;
Ah, why should we lie so curled
Alone in the shell of this great world?
Why should we any more be alone?
Alone, alone, ah woe! alone!

O! 't is a bitter and dreary word,
The saddest by man's ear ever heard;
We each are young, we each have a heart,
Why stand we ever coldly apart?
Must we forever, then, be alone?
Alone, alone, ah woe! alone!

IRENE.

HERS is a spirit deep and crystal-clear;
Calmly beneath her earnest face it lies,
Free without boldness, meek without a fear,
Quicker to look than speak its sympathies;
Far down into her large and patient eyes
I gaze, deep-drinking of the infinite,
As, in the mid-watch of a clear, still night,
I look into the fathomless blue skies.

So circled lives she with Love's holy light,
That from the shade of self she walketh free;
The garden of her soul still keepeth she
An Eden where the snake did never enter;
She hath a natural, wise sincerity,
A simple truthfulness, and these have lent her
A dignity as moveless as the centre;
So that no influence of earth can stir
Her steadfast courage, or can take away
The holy peacefulness, which, night and day,
Unto her queenly soul doth minister.

Most gentle is she; her large charity
(An all unwitting, childlike gift in her)
Not freer is to give than meek to bear;
And, though herself not unacquaint with care,
Hath in her heart wide room for all that be—
Her heart that hath no secrets of its own,
But open is as eglantine full-blown,

Cloudless forever is her brow serene,
Speaking calm hope and trust within her, whence
Welleth a noiseless spring of patience
That keepeth all her life so fresh, so green
And full of holiness, that every look,
The greatness of her woman's soul revealing,
Unto me bringeth blessing, and a feeling
As when I read in God's own holy book.

A graciousness in giving that doth make
The small'st gift greatest, and a sense most meek
Of worthiness, that doth not fear to take
From others, but which always fears to speak
Its thanks in utterance, for the giver's sake ; —
The deep religion of a thankful heart,
Which rests instinctively with Heaven's law
With a full peace, that never can depart
From its own steadfastness ; — a holy awe
For holy things, not those which men call holy,
But such as are revealèd to the eyes
Of a true woman's soul bent down and lowly
Before the face of daily mysteries ; —
A love that blossoms soon, but ripens slowly
To the full goldenness of fruitful prime,
Enduring with a firmness that defies
All shallow tricks of circumstance and time,
By a sure insight knowing where to cling,
And where it clingeth never withering —
These are Irene's dowry — which no fate
Can shake from their serene, deep-builded state.

In-seeing sympathy is hers, which chasteneth
No less than loveth, scorning to be bound
With fear of blame, and yet which ever hasteneth
To pour the balm of kind looks on the wound,
If they be wounds which such sweet teaching makes,
Giving itself a pang for others' sakes;
No want of faith, that chills with side-long eye,
Hath she; no jealousy, no Levite pride
That passeth by upon the other side;
For in her soul there never dwelt a lie,
Right from the hand of God her spirit came
Unstained, and she hath ne'er forgotten whence
It came, nor wandered far from thence,
But laboreth to keep her still the same,
Near to her place of birth, that she may not
Soil her white raiment with an earthly spot.

Yet sets she not her soul so steadily
Above, that she forgets her ties to earth,
But her whole thought would almost seem to be
How to make glad one lowly human hearth;
For with a gentle courage she doth strive
In thought and word and feeling so to live
As to make earth next Heaven; and her heart
Herein doth show its most exceeding worth,
That, bearing in our frailty her just part,
She hath not shrunk from evils of this life,
But hath gone calmly forth into the strife,
And all its sins and sorrows hath withstood
With lofty strength of patient womanhood:

For this I love her great soul more than all,
That, being bound, like us, with earthly thrall,
She walks so bright and Heaven-wise therein —
Too wise, too meek, too womanly to sin.

   Exceeding pleasant to mine eyes is she ;
Like a lone star through riven storm-clouds seen
By sailors, tempest-tost upon the sea,
Telling of rest and peaceful heavens nigh,
Unto my soul her star-like soul hath been,
Her sight as full of hope and calm to me ; —
For she unto herself hath builded high
A home serene, wherein to lay her head,
Earth's noblest thing — a Woman perfected.

THE LOST CHILD.

I.

I WANDERED down the sunny glade
   And ever mused, my love, of thee ;
My thoughts, like little children, played,
   As gayly and as guilelessly.

II.

If any chanced to go astray,
   Moaning in fear of coming harms,
Hope brought the wanderer back alway,
   Safe nestled in her snowy arms.

III.

From that soft nest the happy one
  Looked up at me and calmly smiled;
Its hair shone golden in the sun,
  And made it seem a heavenly child.

IV.

Dear Hope's blue eyes smiled mildly down,
  And blest it with a love so deep,
That, like a nursling of her own,
  It clasped her neck and fell asleep.

THE CHURCH.

I.

I LOVE the rites of England's church;
  I love to hear and see
The priest and people reading slow
  The solemn Litany;
I love to hear the glorious swell
  Of chanted psalm and prayer,
And the deep organ's bursting heart,
  Throb through the shivering air.

II.

Chants, that a thousand years have heard,
   I love to hear again,
For visions of the olden time
   Are wakened by the strain;
With gorgeous hues the window-glass
   Seems suddenly to glow,
And rich and red the streams of light
   Down through the chancel flow.

III.

And then I murmur, " Surely God
   Delighteth here to dwell;
This is the temple of his Son
   Whom he doth love so well; "
But, when I hear the creed which saith,
   This church alone is his,
I feel within my soul that he
   Hath purer shrines than this.

IV.

For His is not the builded church,
   Nor organ-shaken dome ;
In every thing that lovely is
   He loves and hath his home ;

And most in soul that loveth well
    All things which he hath made,
Knowing no creed but simple faith
    That may not be gainsaid.

v.

His church is universal Love,
    And whoso dwells therein
Shall need no customed sacrifice
    To wash away his sin;
And music in its aisles shall swell,
    Of lives upright and true,
Sweet as dreamed sounds of angel-harps
    Down-quivering through the blue.

vi.

They shall not ask a litany,
    The souls that worship there,
But every look shall be a hymn,
    And every word a prayer;
Their service shall be written bright
    In calm and holy eyes,
And every day from fragrant hearts
    Fit incense shall arise.

THE UNLOVELY.

THE pretty things that others wear
Look strange and out of place on me,
I never seem dressed tastefully,
   Because I am not fair;
And, when I would most pleasing seem,
And deck myself with joyful care,
I find it is an idle dream,
   Because I am not fair.

If I put roses in my hair,
They bloom as if in mockery;
Nature denies her sympathy,
   Because I am not fair;
Alas! I have a warm, true heart,
But when I show it people stare;
I must forever dwell apart,
   Because I am not fair.

I am least happy being where
The hearts of others are most light,
And strive to keep me out of sight,
   Because I am not fair;
The glad ones often give a glance,
As I am sitting lonely there,
That asks me why I do not dance —
   Because I am not fair.

And if to smile on them I dare,
For that my heart with love runs o'er,
They say: " What *is* she laughing for?"—
  Because I am not fair;
Love scorned or misinterpreted—
It is the hardest thing to bear;
I often wish that I were dead,
    Because I am not fair.

In joy or grief I must not share,
For neither smiles nor tears on me
Will ever look becomingly,
  Because I am not fair;
Whole days I sit alone and cry,
And in my grave I wish I were—
Yet none will weep me if I die,
    Because I am not fair.

My grave will be so lone and bare,
I fear to think of those dark hours,
For none will plant it o'er with flowers,
  Because I am not fair;
They will not in the summer come
And speak kind words above me there;
To me the grave will be no home,
    Because I am not fair.

LOVE–SONG.

Nearer to thy mother-heart,
Simple Nature, press me,
Let me know thee as thou art,
Fill my soul and bless me!
I have loved thee long and well,
I have loved thee heartily;
Shall I never with thee dwell,
Never be at one with thee?

Inward, inward to thy heart,
Kindly Nature, take me,
Lovely even as thou art,
Full of loving make me!
Thou knowest naught of dead-cold forms,
Knowest naught of littleness,
Lifeful Truth thy being warms,
Majesty and earnestness.

Homeward, homeward to thy heart,
Dearest Nature, call me;
Let no halfness, no mean part,
Any longer thrall me!
I will be thy lover true,
I will be a faithful soul,
Then circle me, then look me through,
Fill me with the mighty Whole.

SONG.

ALL things are sad : —
I go and ask of Memory,
That she tell sweet tales to me
　　To make me glad ;
And she takes me by the hand,
　　Leadeth to old places,
　　Showeth the old faces
In her hazy mirage-land ;
O, her voice is sweet and low,
And her eyes are fresh to mine
　　　　As the dew
　　　　Gleaming through
The half-unfolded eglantine,
Long ago, long ago !
But I feel that I am only
Yet more sad, and yet more lonely !

　　Then I turn to blue-eyed Hope,
And beg of her that she will ope
Her golden gates for me ;
She is fair and full of grace,
But she hath the form and face
Of her mother Memory ;
Clear as air her glad voice ringeth,
Joyous are the songs she singeth,
Yet I hear them mournfully ; —
They are songs her mother taught her,
Crooning to her infant daughter,

As she lay upon her knee.
Many little ones she bore me,
Woe is me! in by-gone hours,
Who danced along and sang before me,
Scattering my way with flowers;
     One by one
     They are gone,
And their silent graves are seen,
Shining fresh with mosses green,
Where the rising sunbeams slope
O'er the dewy land of Hope.

    But, when sweet Memory faileth,
And Hope looks strange and cold;
When youth no more availeth,
And Grief grows over bold; —
When softest winds are dreary,
And summer sunlight weary,
And sweetest things uncheery
     We know not why: —
When the crown of our desires
Weighs upon the brow and tires,
     And we would die,
Die for, ah! we know not what,
Something we seem to have forgot,
Something we had, and now have not; —
When the present is a weight
And the future seems our foe,
And with shrinking eyes we wait,
As one who dreads a sudden blow
In the dark, he knows not whence; —

When Love at last his bright eye closes,
And the bloom upon his face,
That lends him such a living grace,
Is a shadow from the roses
Wherewith we have decked his bier,
Because he once was passing dear ; —
When we feel a leaden sense
Of nothingness and impotence,
    Till we grow mad —
    Then the body saith,
      " There's but one true faith ;
      All things are sad ! "

A LOVE–DREAM.

PLEASANT thoughts come wandering,
When thou art far, from thee to me ;
On their silver wings they bring
A very peaceful ecstasy,
A feeling of eternal spring ;
So that Winter half forgets
Everything but that thou art,
And, in his bewildered heart,
Dreameth of the violets,
Or those bluer flowers that ope,
Flowers of steadfast love and hope,
Watered by the living wells,
Of memories dear, and dearer prophecies,
When young spring forever dwells
In the sunshine of thine eyes.

I have most holy dreams of thee,
    All night I have such dreams;
And, when I wake, reality
    No whit the darker seems;
Through the twin gates of Hope and Memory
    They pour in crystal streams
From out an angel's calmèd eyes,
Who, from twilight till sunrise,
Far away in the upper deep,
Poised upon his shining wings,
Over us his watch doth keep,
And, as he watcheth, ever sings.

Through the still night I hear him sing,
    Down-looking on our sleep;
I hear his clear, clear harp-strings ring,
And, as the golden notes take wing,
Gently downward hovering,
    For very joy I weep;
He singeth songs of holy Love,
That quiver through the depths afar,
Where the blessèd spirits are,
And lingeringly from above
Shower till the morning star
His silver shield hath buckled on
And sentinels the dawn alone,
Quivering his gleamy spear
Through the dusky atmosphere.

Almost, my love, I fear the morn,
When that blessèd voice shall cease,
Lest it should leave me quite forlorn,

Stript of my snowy robe of peace;
And yet the bright reality
Is fairer than all dreams can be,
For, through my spirit, all day long,
Ring echoes of that angel-song
In melodious thoughts of thee;
And well I know it cannot die
Till eternal morn shall break,
For, through life's slumber, thou and I
Will keep it for each other's sake,
And it shall not be silent when we wake.

FOURTH OF JULY ODE.

I.

OUR fathers fought for Liberty,
    They struggled long and well,
    History of their deeds can tell —
But did they leave us free?

II.

Are we free from vanity,
    Free from pride, and free from self,
    Free from love of power and pelf,
From everything that's beggarly?

III.

Are we free from stubborn will,
From low hate and malice small,
From opinion's tyrant thrall?
Are none of us our own slaves still?

IV.

Are we free to speak our thought,
To be happy, and be poor,
Free to enter Heaven's door,
To live and labor as we ought?

V.

Are we then made free at last
From the fear of what men say,
Free to reverence To-day,
Free from the slavery of the Past?

VI.

Our fathers fought for liberty,
They struggled long and well,
History of their deeds can tell —
But *ourselves* must set us free.

SPHINX.

I.

WHY mourn we for the golden prime
When our young souls *were* kingly, strong, and true?
 The soul is greater than all time,
It changes not, but yet is ever new.

II.

But that the soul *is* noble, we
Could never know what nobleness had been;
 Be what ye dream! and earth shall see
A greater greatness than she e'er hath seen.

III.

The flower pines not to be fair,
It never asketh to be sweet and dear,
 But gives itself to sun and air,
And so is fresh and full from year to year.

IV.

Nothing in Nature weeps its lot,
Nothing, save man, abides in memory,
 Forgetful that the Past is what
Ourselves may choose the coming time to be.

v.

All things are circular; the Past
Was given to make the Future great;
    And the void Future shall at last
Be the strong rudder of an after fate.

VI.

We sit beside the Sphinx of Life,
We gaze into its void, unanswering eyes,
    And spend ourselves in idle strife
To read the riddle of their mysteries.

VII.

Arise! be earnest and be strong!
The Sphinx's eyes shall suddenly grow clear,
    And speak as plain to thee ere long,
As the dear maiden's who holds thee most dear.

VIII.

The meaning of all things in *us* —
Yea, in the lives we give our souls — doth lie;
    Make, then, their meaning glorious
By such a life as need not fear to die!

IX.

There is no heart-beat in the day,
Wh.ch bears a record of the smallest deed,
    But holds within its faith alway
That which in doubt we vainly strive to read.

X.

One seed contains another seed,
And that a third, and so for evermore;
    And promise of as great a deed
Lies folded in the deed that went before.

XI.

So ask not fitting space or time,
Yet could not dream of things which could not be;
    Each day shall make the next sublime,
And Time be swallowed in Eternity.

XII.

God bless the Present! it is ALL;
It has been Future, and it shall be Past;
    Awake and live! thy strength recall,
And in one trinity unite them fast.

XIII.

Action and Life — lo! here the key
Of all on earth that seemeth dark and wrong;
    Win this — and, with it, freely ye
May enter that bright realm for which ye long.

XIV.

Then all these bitter questionings
Shall with a full and blessèd answer meet;
    Past worlds, whereof the Poet sings,
Shall be the earth beneath his snow-white fleet.

A PRAYER.

GOD! do not let my loved-one die,
    But rather wait until the time
That I am grown in purity
    Enough to enter thy pure clime,
Then take me, I will gladly go,
So that my love remain below!

O, let her stay! She is by birth
    What I through death must learn to be,
We need her more on our poor earth,
    Than thou canst need in heaven with thee:
She hath her wings already, I
Must burst this earth-shell ere I fly.

Then, God, take me! We shall be near,
    More near than ever, each to each:
Her angel ears will find more clear
    My heavenly than my earthly speech;
And still, as I draw nigh to thee,
Her soul and mine shall closer be.

    1841.

FANTASY.

ROUND and round me she waved swinging,
    Like a wreath of smoke,
In a clear, low gurgle singing
    What may ne'er be spoke;
Her white arms floated on the air,
    Like swans upon a stream,
So stately fair, beyond compare,
    Their gracefulness did seem,
And I knew, by the splendor of her hair,
    That all must be a dream;
For round her limbs it went and came,
        Hither and thither,
        I knew not whither,
Fitfully like a wind-waved flame, —
But bright and golden as flame was never, —
    And it flowed back and forth,
    Like the lights of the north,
Round her and round her forever and ever!

She filled the cup of melody
    With madness to the brim,
And wild, wild songs she sang to me
    That made my brain grow dim,
Like those that throng the traveller's mind,
When night drops down before and behind,
And he can hear naught but the lonely wind
    In the bleak pines over him:
        How may I tell
        The sea-like swell
    Of ever-growing melody,
        That drifted her words,
        Like white sea-birds,
    Swinging and heaving on to me?

Her song came like a sudden breeze;
        It wound through my heart
        With a flashing dart,
    As a bird winds through the trees;
    'T was like a brook flowing,
    'T was like a wind blowing,
    'T was like a star and like a river,
    'T was like all things that weary never, —
    It rhymed with the grass and the open sky,
        With a billowy roll,
        It flooded my soul,
    And thrilled it with fearful ecstasy;
    It was calm as music e'er can be,
    But an inward might was in its motion,
    A consciousness of majesty,

Like the heart of the unruffled ocean,
Which, clear and still, by breeze unshent,
    With a world-wide throe,
    Heaves to and fro
From continent to continent.
  1842.

THE HERITAGE.

THE rich man's son inherits lands,
  And piles of brick, and stone, and gold,
And he inherits soft, white hands,
  And tender flesh that fears the cold,
  Nor dares to wear a garment old;
A heritage, it seems to me,
One scarce would wish to hold in fee.

The rich man's son inherits cares;
  The bank may break, the factory burn,
A breath may burst his bubble shares,
  And soft, white hands could hardly earn
  A living that would serve his turn;
A heritage, it seems to me,
One scarce would wish to hold in fee.

The rich man's son inherits wants,
  His stomach craves for dainty fare;
With sated heart, he hears the pants

Of toiling hinds with brown arms bare,
   And wearies in his easy-chair;
A heritage, it seems to me,
One scarce would wish to hold in fee.

What doth the poor man's son inherit?
   Stout muscles and a sinewy heart,
A hardy frame, a hardier spirit;
   King of two hands, he does his part
   In every useful toil and art;
A heritage, it seems to me,
A king might wish to hold in fee.

What doth the poor man's son inherit?
   Wishes o'erjoyed with humble things,
A rank adjudged by toil-worn merit,
   Content that from employment springs,
   A heart that in his labor sings;
A heritage, it seems to me,
A king might wish to hold in fee.

What doth the poor man's son inherit?
   A patience learned of being poor,
Courage, if sorrow come, to bear it,
   A fellow-feeling that is sure
   To make the outcast bless his door;
A heritage, it seems to me,
A king might wish to hold in fee.

O, rich man's son! there is a toil,
  That with all others level stands;
Large charity doth never soil,
  But only whiten, soft, white hands,
  This is the best crop from thy lands;
A heritage, it seems to me,
Worth being rich to hold in fee.

O, poor man's son! scorn not thy state;
  There is worse weariness than thine,
In merely being rich and great;
  Toil only gives the soul to shine,
  And makes rest fragrant and benign;
A heritage, it seems to me,
Worth being poor to hold in fee.

Both, heirs to some six feet of sod,
  Are equal in the earth at last;
Both, children of the same dear God,
  Prove title to your heirship vast
  By record of a well-filled past;
A heritage, it seems to me,
Well worth a life to hold in fee.

THE ROSE: A BALLAD.

I.

In his tower sat the poet
   Gazing on the roaring sea.
" Take this rose," he sighed, " and throw it
   Where there 's none that loveth me.
On the rock the billow bursteth
   And sinks back into the seas,
But in vain my spirit thirsteth
   So to burst and be at ease.
Take, O, sea! the tender blossom
   That hath lain against my breast;
On thy black and angry bosom
   It will find a surer rest.
Life is vain, and love is hollow,
   Ugly death stands there behind,
Hate and scorn and hunger follow
   Him that toileth for his kind."
Forth into the night he hurled it,
   And with bitter smile did mark
How the surly tempest whirled it
   Swift into the hungry dark.
Foam and spray drive back to leeward,
   And the gale, with dreary moan,
Drifts the helpless blossom seaward,
   Through the breakers all alone.

II.

Stands a maiden, on the morrow,
   Musing by the wave-beat strand,
Half in hope and half in sorrow,
   Tracing words upon the sand:
" Shall I ever then behold him
   Who hath been my life so long,—
Ever to this sick heart fold him,—
   Be the spirit of his song?
Touch not, sea, the blessed letters
   I have traced upon thy shore,
Spare his name whose spirit fetters
   Mine with love forevermore!"
Swells the tide and overflows it,
   But, with omen pure and meet,
Brings a little rose, and throws it
   Humbly at the maiden's feet.
Full of bliss she takes the token,
   And, upon her snowy breast,
Soothes the ruffled petals broken
   With the ocean's fierce unrest.
" Love is thine, O, heart! and surely
   Peace shall also be thine own,
For the heart that trusteth purely
   Never long can pine alone."

III.

In his tower sits the poet,
  Blisses new and strange to him
Fill his heart and overflow it
  With a wonder sweet and dim.
Up the beach the ocean slideth
  With a whisper of delight,
And the moon in silence glideth
  Through the peaceful blue of night.
Rippling o'er the poet's shoulder
  Flows a maiden's golden hair,
Maiden-lips, with love grown bolder,
  Kiss his moon-lit forehead bare.
" Life is joy, and love is power,
  Death all fetters doth unbind,
Strength and wisdom only flower
  When we toil for all our kind.
Hope is truth, — the future giveth
  More than present takes away,
And the soul forever liveth
  Nearer God from day to day."
Not a word the maiden uttered,
  Fullest hearts are slow to speak,
But a withered roseleaf fluttered
  Down upon the poet's cheek.

  1842.

ELEGY ON THE DEATH OF DR. CHANNING.

I DO not come to weep above thy pall,
  And mourn the dying-out of noble powers;
The poet's clearer eye should see, in all
  Earth's seeming woe, the seed of Heaven's flowers.

Truth needs no champions: in the infinite deep
  Of everlasting Soul her strength abides,
From Nature's heart her mighty pulses leap,
  Through Nature's veins her strength, undying,
    tides.

Peace is more strong than war, and gentleness,
  Where force were vain, makes conquests o'er the
    wave;
And love lives on and hath a power to bless,
  When they who loved are hidden in the grave.

The sculptured marble brags of death-strewn fields,
  And Glory's epitaph is writ in blood;
But Alexander now to Plato yields,
  Clarkson will stand where Wellington hath stood.

I watch the circle of the eternal years,
  And read forever in the storied page
One lengthened roll of blood, and wrong, and tears,
  One onward step of Truth from age to age.

The poor are crushed; the tyrants link their chain;
  The poet sings through narrow dungeon-grates;
Man's hope lies quenched; — and, lo! with steadfast
      gain
  Freedom doth forge her mail of adverse fates.

Men slay the prophets; fagot, rack, and cross
  Make up the groaning record of the past;
But Evil's triumphs are her endless loss,
  And sovereign Beauty wins the soul at last.

No power can die that ever wrought for Truth;
  Thereby a law of Nature it became,
And lives unwithered in its sinewy youth,
  When he who called it forth is but a name.

Therefore I cannot think thee wholly gone;
  The better part of thee is with us still;
Thy soul its hampering clay aside hath thrown,
  And only freer wrestles with the Ill.

Thou livest in the life of all good things;
  What words thou spak'st for Freedom shall not die;
Thou sleepest not, for now thy Love hath wings
  To soar where hence thy Hope could hardly fly.

And often, from that other world, on this
  Some gleams from great souls gone before may
      shine,
To shed on struggling hearts a clearer bliss,
  And clothe the Right with lustre more divine.

Thou art not idle : in thy higher sphere
   Thy spirit bends itself to loving tasks,
And strength, to perfect what it dreamed of here,
   Is all the crown and glory that it asks.

For sure, in Heaven's wide chambers, there is room
   For love and pity, and for helpful deeds ;
Else were our summons thither but a doom
   To life more vain than this in clayey weeds.

From off the starry mountain-peak of song,
   Thy spirit shows me, in the coming time,
An earth unwithered by the foot of wrong,
   A race revering its own soul sublime.

What wars, what martyrdoms, what crimes, may come
   Thou knowest not, nor I ; but God will lead
The prodigal soul from want and sorrow home,
   And Eden ope her gates to Adam's seed.

Farewell ! good man, good angel now ! this hand
   Soon, like thine own, shall lose its cunning, too ;
Soon shall this soul, like thine, bewildered stand,
   Then leap to thread the free, unfathomed blue :

When that day comes, O, may this hand grow cold,
   Busy, like thine, for Freedom and the Right ;
O, may this soul, like thine, be ever bold
   To face dark Slavery's encroaching blight !

This laurel-leaf I cast upon thy bier;
   Let worthier hands than these thy wreath entwine;
Upon thy hearse I shed no useless tear, —
   For me weep rather thou in calm divine!
    1842.

STANZAS.

SUNG AT THE ANTI-SLAVERY PICNIC IN DEDHAM, ON THE ANNIVER-
SARY OF WEST-INDIA EMANCIPATION, AUGUST 1, 1843.

MEN! whose boast it is that ye
Come of fathers brave and free,
If there breathe on earth a slave,
Are ye truly free and brave?
If ye do not feel the chain,
When it works a brother's pain,
Are ye not base slaves indeed, —
Slaves unworthy to be freed?

Women! who shall one day bear
Sons to breathe New England air,
If ye hear, without a blush,
Deeds to make the roused blood rush
Like red lava through your veins,
For your sisters now in chains, —
Answer! are ye fit to be
Mothers of the brave and free?

Is true Freedom but to break
Fetters for our own dear sake,
And, with leathern hearts, forget
That we owe mankind a debt?
No! true freedom is to share
All the chains our brothers wear,
And, with heart and hand, to be
Earnest to make others free!

They are slaves who fear to speak
For the fallen and the weak;
They are slaves who will not choose
Hatred, scoffing, and abuse,
Rather than in silence shrink
From the truth they needs must think;
They are slaves who dare not be
In the right with two or three.

———

SILENCE.

WHEN the cup of hope brims over
  And the soul hath drunk its fill,
When the loved-one meets the lover
And their hearts in sunshine hover
  With one impulse and one will, —
  Then the useless tongue is still.

When the heart is bare of gladness,
  And the helpless sense of ill
Goads the apathy of sadness
Onward, through a whirl of madness
  To a darkness drear and chill, —
  Then the palsied tongue is still.

When the soul for power sigheth,
  Struggling for Art's fuller skill,
And the prophet heart o'erflieth
All the agony that trieth,
  All the teardrops it must spill, —
  Then the trancèd tongue is still.

When two hearts that love are parted,
  And truth lingers but to kill,
When they strive to be hardhearted,
And the props of life are started
  With a terror and a thrill, —
  Then the choking tongue is still.

When our souls youth's dream-chains shiver,
  And we leap the world's scant rill,
Which had seemed a mighty river
Roaring on and on forever
  'Tween us and Self-trust's steep hill, —
  Then the trembling tongue is still.

O, sweet Silence! they belied thee
  Who have called thee vain and weak;
Speech is emptiness beside thee,

Joy and woe have glorified thee,
    Love and longing never seek
    Any better way to speak.

All the deepest thoughts and feelings
    Which the roots of life enfold,
Passion's sudden shocks and reelings,
Love's first tremulous revealings,
    Never can be fully told,
    Save by thee, revered of old!

A CHIPPEWA LEGEND.[1]

ἀλγεινὰ μέν μοι καὶ λέγειν ἐστὶν τάδε
ἄλγος δὲ σιγᾶν.

        Æschylus, Prom. Vinct. 197.

THE old Chief, feeling now well-nigh his end,
Called his two eldest children to his side,
And gave them, in few words, his parting charge:
"My son and daughter, me ye see no more;
The happy hunting-grounds await me, green
With change of spring and summer through the year:
But, for remembrance, after I am gone,
Be kind to little Sheemah for my sake:
Weakling he is and young, and knows not yet
To set the trap, or draw the seasoned bow;

[1] For the leading incidents in this tale, I am indebted to the very valuable "Algic Researches" of Henry R. Schoolcraft, Esq.

Therefore of both your loves he hath more need,
And he, who needeth love, to love hath right;
It is not like our furs and stores of corn,
Whereto we claim sole title by our toil,
But the Great Spirit plants it in our hearts,
And waters it, and gives it sun, to be
The common stock and heritage of all:
Therefore be kind to Sheemah, that yourselves
May not be left deserted in your need."

Alone, beside a lake, their wigwam stood,
Far from the other dwellings of their tribe;
And, after many moons, the loneliness
Wearied the elder brother, and he said,
"Why should I dwell here all alone, shut out
From the free, natural joys that fit my age?
Lo, I am tall and strong, well skilled to hunt,
Patient of toil and hunger, and not yet
Have seen the danger which I dared not look
Full in the face; what hinders me to be
A mighty Brave and Chief among my kin?"
So, taking up his arrows and his bow,
As if to hunt, he journeyed swiftly on,
Until he gained the wigwams of his tribe,
Where, choosing out a bride, he soon forgot,
In all the fret and bustle of new life,
The little Sheemah and his father's charge.

Now when the sister found her brother gone,
And that, for many days, he came not back,
She wept for Sheemah more than for herself;
For Love bides longest in a woman's heart,

And flutters many times before he flies,
And then doth perch so nearly, that a word
May lure him back, as swift and glad as light;
And Duty lingers even when Love is gone,
Oft looking out in hope of his return;
And after Duty hath been driven forth,
Then Selfishness creeps in the last of all,
Warming her lean hands at the lonely hearth,
And crouching o'er the embers, to shut out
Whatever paltry warmth and light are left,
With avaricious greed, from all beside.
So, for long months, the sister hunted wide,
And cared for little Sheemah tenderly;
But, daily more and more, the loneliness
Grew wearisome, and to herself she sighed,
"Am I not fair? at least the glassy pool,
That hath no cause to flatter, tells me so;
But, O, how flat and meaningless the tale,
Unless it tremble on a lover's tongue!
Beauty hath no true glass, except it be
In the sweet privacy of loving eyes."
Thus deemed she idly, and forgot the lore
Which she had learned of nature and the woods,
That beauty's chief reward is to itself,
And that the eyes of Love reflect alone
The inward fairness, which is blurred and lost
Unless kept clear and white by Duty's care.
So she went forth and sought the haunts of men,
And, being wedded, in her household cares,
Soon, like the elder brother, quite forgot
The little Sheemah and her father's charge.

But Sheemah, left alone within the lodge,
Waited and waited, with a shrinking heart,
Thinking each rustle was his sister's step,
Till hope grew less and less, and then went out,
And every sound was changed from hope to fear.
Few sounds there were: — the dropping of a nut,
The squirrel's chirrup, and the jay's harsh scream,
Autumn's sad remnants of blithe Summer's cheer,
Heard at long intervals, seemed but to make
The dreadful void of silence silenter.
Soon what small store his sister left was gone,
And, through the Autumn, he made shift to live
On roots and berries, gathered in much fear
Of wolves, whose ghastly howl he heard ofttimes,
Hollow and hungry, at the dead of night.
But Winter came at last, and, when the snow,
Thick-heaped for gleaming leagues o'er hill and plain,
Spread its unbroken silence over all,
Made bold by hunger, he was fain to glean,
(More sick at heart than Ruth, and all alone,)
After the harvest of the merciless wolf,
Grim Boaz, who, sharp-ribbed and gaunt, yet feared
A thing more wild and starving than himself;
Till, by degrees, the wolf and he grew friends,
And shared together all the winter through.

Late in the Spring, when all the ice was gone,
The elder brother, fishing in the lake,
Upon whose edge his father's wigwam stood,
Heard a low moaning noise upon the shore:
Half like a child it seemed, half like a wolf,
And straightway there was something in his heart

That said, " It is thy brother Sheemah's voice."
So, paddling swiftly to the bank, he saw,
Within a little thicket close at hand,
A child that seemed fast changing to a wolf,
From the neck downward, gray with shaggy hair,
That still crept on and upward as he looked.
The face was turned away, but well he knew
That it was Sheemah's, even his brother's face.
Then with his trembling hands he hid his eyes,
And bowed his head, so that he might not see
The first look of his brother's eyes, and cried,
" O, Sheemah! O, my brother, speak to me!
Dost thou not know me, that I am thy brother?
Come to me, little Sheemah, thou shalt dwell
With me henceforth, and know no care or want!"
Sheemah was silent for a space, as if
'T were hard to summon up a human voice,
And, when he spake, the sound was of a wolf's:
" I know thee not, nor art thou what thou sayest;
I have none other brethren than the wolves,
And, till thy heart be changed from what it is,
Thou art not worthy to be called their kin."
Then groaned the other, with a choking tongue,
" Alas! my heart is changed right bitterly;
'T is shrunk and parched within me even now!"
And, looking upward fearfully, he saw
Only a wolf that shrank away and ran,
Ugly and fierce, to hide among the woods.

This rude, wild legend hath an inward sense,
Which it were well we all should lay to heart;
For have not we our younger brothers, too,

The poor, the outcast, and the trodden-down,
Left fatherless on earth to pine for bread?
They are ahungered for our love and care,
It is their spirits that are famishing,
And our dear Father, in his Testament,
Bequeathed them to us as our dearest trust,
Whereof we shall give up a straight account.
Woe, if we have forgotten them, and left
Those souls that might have grown so fair and glad,
That only wanted a kind word from us,
To be so free and gently beautiful, —
Left them to feel their birthright as a curse,
To grow all lean, and cramped, and full of sores,
And last, — sad change, that surely comes to all
Shut out from manhood by their brother-man, —
To turn mere wolves, for lack of aught to love!

Hear it, O England! thou who liest asleep
On a volcano, from whose pent-up wrath,
Already some red flashes, bursting up,
Glare bloodily on coronet and crown
And gray cathedral looming huge aloof,
With dreadful portent of o'erhanging doom!
Thou Dives among nations! from whose board,
After the dogs are fed, poor Lazarus,
Crooked and worn with toil, and hollow-eyed,
Begs a few crumbs in vain!
                                    I honor thee
For all the lessons thou hast taught the world,
Not few nor poor, and freedom chief of all;
I honor thee for thy huge energy,

Thy tough endurance, and thy fearless heart:
And how could man, who speaks with English words,
Think lightly of the blessed womb that bare
Shakspeare and Milton, and full many more
Whose names are now our earth's sweet lullabies,
Wherewith she cheers the infancy of those
Who are to do her honor in their lives?
Yet I would bid thee, ere too late, beware,
Lest, while thou playest off thine empty farce
Of Queenship to outface a grinning world,
Patching thy purple out with filthy rags,
To make thy madness a more bitter scoff,
Thy starving millions, — who not only pine
For body's bread, but for the bread of life,
The light, which from their eyes is quite shut out
By the broad mockery of thy golden roof, —
Should turn to wolves that hanker for thy blood.
Even now their cry, which, o'er the ocean-stream,
Wanders, and moans upon the awe-struck ear,
Clear-heard above the sea's eternal wail,
But deeper far, and mournfuller, than that,
(For naught so fathomless as woe unshared,)
Hath learned a savage meaning of the wolf,
Whose nature now half-triumphs in the heart
Of the world-exiled and despairing Man.

And thou, my country, who to me art dear
As is the blood that circles through my heart,
To whom God granted it in charge to be
Freedom's apostle to a trampled world,
Who shouldst have been a mighty name to shake

Old lies and shams, as with a voice from Heaven,
Art little better than a sneer and mock,
And tyrants smile to see thee holding up
Freedom's broad Ægis o'er three million slaves!
Shall God forget himself to humor thee?
Shall Justice lie to screen thine ugly sin?
Shall the eternal laws of truth become
Cobwebs to let thy foul oppression through?
Shall the untiring Vengeance, that pursues,
Age after age, upon the sinner's track,
Roll back his burning deluge at thy beck?
Woe! woe! Even now I see thy star drop down,
Waning and pale, its faint disc flecked with blood,
That had been set in heaven gloriously,
To beacon Man to Freedom and to Home!
Woe! woe! I hear the loathsome serpent hiss,
Trailing, unharmed, its slow and bloated folds
O'er the lone ruins of thy Capitol!
I see those outcast millions turned to wolves,
That howl and snarl o'er Freedom's gory corse,
And lap the ebbing heart's-blood of that Hope,
Which would have made our earth smile back on
        heaven,
A happy child upon a happy mother,
From whose ripe breast it drew the milk of life.

But no, my country! other thoughts than these
Befit a son of thine: serener thoughts
Befit the heart which can, unswerved, believe
That Wrong already feels itself o'ercome,
If but one soul have strength to see the right,

Or one free tongue dare speak it. All mankind
Look, with an anxious flutter of the heart,
To see thee working out thy glorious doom.
Thou shalt not, with a lie upon thy lips,
Forever prop up cunning despotisms,
And help to strengthen every tyrant's plea,
By striving to make man's deep soul content
With a half-truth that feeds it with mere wind.
God judgeth us by what we know of right,
Rather than what we practise that is wrong,
Unknowingly; and thou shalt yet be bold
To stand before Him, with a heart made clean
By doing that He taught thee how to preach.
Thou yet shalt do thy holy errand; yet,
That little Mayflower, convoyed by the winds
And the rude waters to our rocky shore,
Shall scatter Freedom's seed throughout the world,
And all the nations of the earth shall come,
Singing, to share the harvest-home of Truth.

———————

THE VISION OF SIR LAUNFAL.

PRELUDE TO PART FIRST.

Over his keys the musing organist,
  Beginning doubtfully and far away,
First lets his fingers wander as they list,
  And builds a bridge from Dreamland for his lay;

Then, as the touch of his loved instrument
  Gives hope and fervor, nearer draws his theme,
First guessed by faint auroral flushes sent
  Along the wavering vista of his dream.

  Not only around our infancy
  Doth heaven with all its splendors lie;
  Daily, with souls that cringe and plot,
  We Sinais climb and know it not;

Over our manhood bend the skies;
  Against our fallen and traitor lives
The great winds utter prophecies;
  With our faint hearts the mountain strives;
Its arms outstretched, the druid wood
  Waits with its benedicite;
And to our age's drowsy blood
  Still shouts the inspiring sea.

Earth gets its price for what Earth gives us;
  The beggar is taxed for a corner to die in,
The priest hath his fee who comes and shrives us,
  We bargain for the graves we lie in;
At the Devil's booth are all things sold,
Each ounce of dross costs its ounce of gold;
  For a cap and bells our lives we pay,
Bubbles we earn with a whole soul's tasking:
  'T is heaven alone that is given away,
'T is only God may be had for the asking;
There is no price set on the lavish summer;
And June may be had by the poorest comer.

And what is so rare as a day in June?
  Then, if ever, come perfect days;
Then Heaven tries the earth if it be in tune,
  And over it softly her warm ear lays:
Whether we look, or whether we listen,
We hear life murmur, or see it glisten;
Every clod feels a stir of might,
  An instinct within it that reaches and towers,
And, grasping blindly above it for light,
  Climbs to a soul in grass and flowers;
The flush of life may well be seen
  Thrilling back over hills and valleys;
The cowslip startles in meadows green,
  The buttercup catches the sun in its chalice,
And there 's never a leaf or a blade too mean
  To be some happy creature's palace;
The little bird sits at his door in the sun,
  Atilt like a blossom among the leaves,
And lets his illumined being o'errun
  With the deluge of summer it receives;
His mate feels the eggs beneath her wings,
And the heart in her dumb breast flutters and sings;
He sings to the wide world, and she to her nest, —
In the nice ear of Nature which song is the best?

Now is the high-tide of the year,
  And whatever of life hath ebbed away
Comes flooding back, with a ripply cheer,
  Into every bare inlet and creek and bay;
Now the heart is so full that a drop overfills it,
We are happy now because God so wills it;

No matter how barren the past may have been,
'T is enough for us now that the leaves are green;
We sit in the warm shade and feel right well
How the sap creeps up and the blossoms swell;
We may shut our eyes, but we cannot help knowing
That skies are clear and grass is growing;
The breeze comes whispering in our ear,
That dandelions are blossoming near,
   That maize has sprouted, that streams are flowing,
That the river is bluer than the sky,
That the robin is plastering his house hard by;
And if the breeze kept the good news back,
For other couriers we should not lack;
   We could guess it all by yon heifer's lowing, —
And hark! how clear bold chanticleer,
Warmed with the new wine of the year,
   Tells all in his lusty crowing!

Joy comes, grief goes, we know not how;
Everything is happy now,
   Everything is upward striving;
'T is as easy now for the heart to be true
As for grass to be green or skies to be blue, —
   'T is the natural way of living:
Who knows whither the clouds have fled?
   In the unscarred heaven they leave no wake;
And the eyes forget the tears they have shed,
   The heart forgets its sorrow and ache;
The soul partakes the season's youth,
   And the sulphurous rifts of passion and woe

Lie deep 'neath a silence pure and smooth,
   Like burnt-out craters healed with snow.
What wonder if Sir Launfal now
Remembered the keeping of his vow?

PART FIRST.

I.

" My golden spurs now bring to me,
   And bring to me my richest mail,
For to-morrow I go over land and sea
   In search of the Holy Grail;
Shall never a bed for me be spread,
Nor shall a pillow be under my head,
Till I begin my vow to keep;
Here on the rushes will I sleep,
And perchance there may come a vision true
Ere day create the world anew."
   Slowly Sir Launfal's eyes grew dim,
   Slumber fell like a cloud on him,
And into his soul the vision flew.

II.

The crows flapped over by twos and threes,
In the pool drowsed the cattle up to their knees,
   The little birds sang as if it were
   The one day of summer in all the year,
And the very leaves seemed to sing on the trees:

The castle alone in the landscape lay
Like an outpost of winter, dull and gray;
'T was the proudest hall in the North Countree,
And never its gates might opened be,
Save to lord or lady of high degree;
Summer besieged it on every side,
But the churlish stone her assaults defied;
She could not scale the chilly wall,
Though around it for leagues her pavilions tall
Stretched left and right,
Over the hills and out of sight;
  Green and broad was every tent,
  And out of each a murmur went
Till the breeze fell off at night.

III.

The drawbridge dropped with a surly clang,
And through the dark arch a charger sprang,
Bearing Sir Launfal, the maiden knight,
In his gilded mail, that flamed so bright
It seemed the dark castle had gathered all
Those shafts the fierce sun had shot over its wall
  In his siege of three hundred summers long,
And, binding them all in one blazing sheaf,
  Had cast them forth: so, young and strong,
And lightsome as a locust-leaf,
Sir Launfal flashed forth in his unscarred mail,
To seek in all climes for the Holy Grail.

IV.

It was morning on hill and stream and tree,
   And morning in the young knight's heart;
Only the castle moodily
Rebuffed the gifts of the sunshine free.
   And gloomed by itself apart;
The season brimmed all other things up
Full as the rain fills the pitcher-plant's cup.

V.

As Sir Launfal made morn through the darksome
    gate,
   He was ware of a leper, crouched by the same,
Who begged with his hand and moaned as he
    sate;
   And a loathing over Sir Launfal came;
The sunshine went out of his soul with a thrill,
   The flesh 'neath his armor did shrink and crawl,
And midway its leap his heart stood still
   Like a frozen waterfall;
For this man, so foul and bent of stature,
Rasped harshly against his dainty nature,
And seemed the one blot on the summer morn, —
So he tossed him a piece of gold in scorn.

VI.

The leper raised not the gold from the dust:
" Better to me the poor man's crust,
Better the blessing of the poor,
Though I turn me empty from his door;
That is no true alms which the hand can hold;
He gives nothing but worthless gold
   Who gives from a sense of duty;
But he who gives but a slender mite,
And gives to that which is out of sight,
   That thread of the all-sustaining Beauty
Which runs through all and doth all unite, —
The hand cannot clasp the whole of his alms,
The heart outstretches its eager palms,
For a god goes with it and makes it store
To the soul that was starving in darkness before."

PRELUDE TO PART SECOND.

DOWN swept the chill wind from the mountain peak,
   From the snow five thousand summers old;
On open wold and hill-top bleak
   It had gathered all the cold,
And whirled it like sleet on the wanderer's cheek;
It carried a shiver everywhere
From the unleafed boughs and pastures bare;

The little brook heard it and built a roof
'Neath which he could house him, winter-proof;
All night by the white stars' frosty gleams
He groined his arches and matched his beams;
Slender and clear were his crystal spars
As the lashes of light that trim the stars:
He sculptured every summer delight
In his halls and chambers out of sight;
Sometimes his tinkling waters slipt
Down through a frost-leaved forest-crypt,
Long, sparkling aisles of steel-stemmed trees
Bending to counterfeit a breeze;
Sometimes the roof no fretwork knew
But silvery mosses that downward grew;
Sometimes it was carved in sharp relief
With quaint arabesques of ice-fern leaf;
Sometimes it was simply smooth and clear
For the gladness of heaven to shine through, and
     here
He had caught the nodding bulrush-tops
And hung them thickly with diamond drops,
That crystalled the beams of moon and sun,
And made a star of every one:
No mortal builder's most rare device
Could match this winter-palace of ice;
'T was as if every image that mirrored lay
In his depths serene through the summer day,
Each fleeting shadow of earth and sky,
  Lest the happy model should be lost,
Had been mimicked in fairy masonry
  By the elfin builders of the frost.

Within the hall are song and laughter,
  The cheeks of Christmas glow red and jolly,
And sprouting is every corbel and rafter
  With lightsome green of ivy and holly;
Through the deep gulf of the chimney wide
Wallows the Yule-log's roaring tide;
The broad flame-pennons droop and flap
  And belly and tug as a flag in the wind;
Like a locust shrills the imprisoned sap,
  Hunted to death in its galleries blind;
And swift little troops of silent sparks,
  Now pausing, now scattering away as in fear,
Go threading the soot-forest's tangled darks
  Like herds of startled deer.

But the wind without was eager and sharp,
Of Sir Launfal's gray hair it makes a harp,
    And rattles and wrings
    The icy strings,
  Singing, in dreary monotone,
  A Christmas carol of its own,
  Whose burden still, as he might guess,
  Was — "Shelterless, shelterless, shelterless!"
The voice of the seneschal flared like a torch
As he shouted the wanderer away from the porch,
And he sat in the gateway and saw all night
  The great hall-fire so cheery and bold,
  Through the window-slits of the castle old,
Build out its piers of ruddy light
Against the drift of the cold.

PART SECOND

I.

There was never a leaf on bush or tree,
The bare boughs rattled shudderingly;
The river was dumb and could not speak,
  For the frost's swift shuttles its shroud had spun;
A single crow on the tree-top bleak
  From his shining feathers shed off the cold sun;
Again it was morning, but shrunk and cold,
As if her veins were sapless and old,
And she rose up decrepitly
For a last dim look at earth and sea.

II.

Sir Launfal turned from his own hard gate,
For another heir in his earldom sate;
An old, bent man, worn out and frail,
He came back from seeking the Holy Grail;
Little he recked of his earldom's loss,
No more on his surcoat was blazoned the cross,
But deep in his soul the sign he wore,
The badge of the suffering and the poor.

III.

Sir Launfal's raiment thin and spare
Was idle mail 'gainst the barbèd air,
For it was just at the Christmas time;
So he mused, as he sat, of a sunnier clime,
And sought for a shelter from cold and snow
In the light and warmth of long ago;
He sees the snake-like caravan crawl
O'er the edge of the desert, black and small,
Then nearer and nearer, till, one by one
He can count the camels in the sun,
As over the red-hot sands they pass
To where, in its slender necklace of grass,
The little spring laughed and leapt in the shade,
And with its own self like an infant played,
And waved its signal of palms.

IV.

"For Christ's sweet sake, I beg an alms;"—
The happy camels may reach the spring,
But Sir Launfal sees naught save the grewsome thing,
The leper, lank as the rain-blanched bone,
That cowers beside him, a thing as lone
And white as the ice-isles of Northern seas
In the desolate horror of his disease.

V.

And Sir Launfal said, — " I behold in thee
An image of Him who died on the tree ;
Thou also hast had thy crown of thorns, —
Thou also hast had the world's buffets and scorns, —
And to thy life were not denied
The wounds in the hands and feet and side :
Mild Mary's Son, acknowledge me ;
Behold, through him, I give to thee ! "

VI.

Then the soul of the leper stood up in his eyes
    And looked at Sir Launfal, and straightway he
Remembered in what a haughtier guise
    He had flung an alms to leprosie,
When he caged his young life up in gilded mail
And set forth in search of the Holy Grail.
The heart within him was ashes and dust ;
He parted in twain his single crust,
He broke the ice on the streamlet's brink,
And gave the leper to eat and drink,
'T was a mouldy crust of coarse brown bread,
    'T was water out of a wooden bowl, —
Yet with fine wheaten bread was the leper fed,
    And 't was red wine he drank with his thirsty soul.

VII.

As Sir Launfal mused with a downcast face,
A light shone round about the place;
The leper no longer crouched at his side,
But stood before him glorified,
Shining and tall and fair and straight
As the pillar that stood by the Beautiful Gate, —
Himself the Gate whereby men can
Enter the temple of God in Man.

VIII.

His words were shed softer than leaves from the pine,
And they fell on Sir Launfal as snows on the brine,
That mingle their softness and quiet in one
With the shaggy unrest they float down upon;
And the voice that was calmer than silence said,
" Lo it is I, be not afraid!
In many climes, without avail,
Thou hast spent thy life for the Holy Grail;
Behold, it is here, — this cup which thou
Didst fill at the streamlet for me but now;
This crust is my body broken for thee,
This water His blood that died on the tree;
The Holy Supper is kept, indeed,
In whatso we share with another's need;
Not what we give, but what we share, —
For the gift without the giver is bare;
Who gives himself with his alms feeds three, —
Himself, his hungering neighbor, and me."

" And the voice that was calmer than silence said
' Lo it is I, be not afraid ! ' "

IX.

Sir Launfal awoke as from a swound : —
" The Grail in my castle here is found !
Hang my idle armor up on the wall,
Let it be the spider's banquet-hall ;
He must be fenced with stronger mail
Who would seek and find the Holy Grail."

X.

The castle gate stands open now,
   And the wanderer is welcome to the hall
As the hangbird is to the elm-tree bough ;
   No longer scowl the turrets tall,
The summer's long siege at last is o'er ;
When the first poor outcast went in at the door,
She entered with him in disguise,
And mastered the fortress by surprise ;
There is no spot she loves so well on ground,
She lingers and smiles there the whole year round ;
The meanest serf on Sir Launfal's land
Has hall and bower at his command ;
And there 's no poor man in the North Countree
But is lord of the earldom as much as he.

NOTE. — According to the mythology of the Romancers, the San
Greal, or Holy Grail, was the cup out of which Jesus partook of the
last supper with his disciples. It was brought into England by Joseph
of Arimathea, and remained there, an object of pilgrimage and adora-
tion, for many years in the keeping of his lineal descendants. It was

SONNETS.

I.

DISAPPOINTMENT.

I PRAY thee call not this society;
I asked for bread, thou givest me a stone;
I am an hungered, and I find not one
To give me meat, to joy or grieve with me;
I find not here what I went out to see —
Souls of true men, of women who can move
The deeper, better part of us to love,
Souls that can hold with mine communion free.
Alas! must then these hopes, these longings high,
This yearning of the soul for brotherhood,
And all that makes us pure, and wise, and good,
Come broken-hearted, home again to die?
No, Hope is left, and prays with bended head,
"Give us this day, O God, our daily bread!"

---

incumbent upon those who had charge of it to be chaste in thought,
word, and deed; but one of the keepers having broken this condi-
tion, the Holy Grail disappeared. From that time it was a favorite
enterprise of the knights of Arthur's court to go in search of it.
Sir Galahad was at last successful in finding it, as may be read in the
seventeenth book of the Romance of King Arthur. Tennyson has
made Sir Galahad the subject of one of the most exquisite of his
poems.

The plot (if I may give that name to anything so slight) of the
foregoing poem is my own, and, to serve its purposes, I have enlarged
the circle of competition in search of the miraculous cup in such
a manner as to include, not only other persons than the heroes of the
Round Table, but also a period of time subsequent to the date of
King Arthur's reign.

II.

GREAT human nature, whither art thou fled?
Are these things creeping forth and back agen,
These hollow formalists and echoes, men?
Art thou entombèd with the mighty dead?
In God's name, no! not yet hath all been said,
Or done, or longed for, that is truly great;
These pitiful dried crusts will never sate
Natures for which pure Truth is daily bread;
We were not meant to plod along the earth,
Strange to ourselves and to our fellows strange;
We were not meant to struggle from our birth
To skulk and creep, and in mean pathways range;
Act! with stern truth, large faith, and loving will!
Up and be doing! God is with us still.

III.

TO A FRIEND.

ONE strip of bark may feed the broken tree,
Giving to some few limbs a sickly green;
And one light shower on the hills, I ween,
May keep the spring from drying utterly.
Thus seemeth it with these our hearts to be;
Hope is the strip of bark, the shower of rain,
And so they are not wholly crushed with pain.
But live and linger on, for sadder sight to see;
Much do they err, who tell us that the heart

May not be broken; what, then, can we call
A broken heart, if this may not be so,
This death in life, when, shrouded in its pall,
Shunning and shunned, it dwelleth all apart,
Its power, its love, its sympathy laid low?

IV.

So may it be, but let it not be so,
O, let it not be so with thee, my friend;
Be of good courage, bear up to the end,
And on thine after way rejoicing go!
We all must suffer, if we aught would know;
Life is a teacher stern, and wisdom's crown
Is oft a crown of thorns, whence, trickling down,
Blood, mixed with tears, blinding her eyes doth flow;
But Time, a gentle nurse, shall wipe away
This bloody sweat, and thou shalt find on earth,
That woman is not all in all to Love,
But, living by a new and second birth,
Thy soul shall see all things below, above,
Grow bright and brighter to the perfect day.

V.

O CHILD of Nature! O most meek and free,
Most gentle spirit of true nobleness!
Thou doest not a worthy deed the less
Because the world may not its greatness see;
What were a thousand triumphings to thee,
Who, in thyself, art as a perfect sphere

Wrapt in a bright and natural atmosphere
Of mighty-souledness and majesty?
Thy soul is not too high for lowly things,
Feels not its strength seeing its brother weak,
Nor for itself unto itself is dear,
But for that it may guide the wanderings
Of fellow-men, and to their spirits speak
The lofty faith of heart that knows no fear.

VI.

"For this true nobleness I seek in vain,
In woman and in man I find it not,
I almost weary of my earthly lot,
My life-strings are dried up with burning pain." —
Thou find'st it not?   I pray thee look again,
Look *inward* through the depths of thine own soul;
How is it with thee?   Art thou sound and whole?
Doth narrow search show thee no earthly stain?
Be noble! and the nobleness that lies
In other men, sleeping but never dead,
Will rise in majesty to meet thine own;
Then wilt thou see it gleam in many eyes,
Then will pure light around thy path be shed,
And thou wilt nevermore be sad and lone.

VII.

TO ———

Deem it no Sodom-fruit of vanity,
Or fickle fantasy of unripe youth
Which ever takes the fairest shows for truth,

That I should wish my verse beloved of thee;
'T is love's deep thirst which may not quenchèd be.
There is a gulf of longing and unrest,
A wild love-craving not to be represt,
Whereto, in all our hearts, as to the sea,
The streams of feeling do for ever flow.
Therefore it is that thy well-meted praise
Falleth so shower-like and fresh on me,
Filling those springs which else had sunk full low,
Lost in the dreary desert-sands of woe,
Or parched by passion's fierce and withering blaze.

VIII.

MIGHT I but be beloved, and, O most fair
And perfect-ordered soul, beloved of thee,
How should I feel a cloud of earthly care,
If thy blue eyes were ever clear to me?
O woman's love! O flower most bright and rare!
That blossom'st brightest in extremest need,
Woe, woe is me! that thy so precious seed
Is ever sown by Fancy's changeful air,
And grows sometimes in poor and barren hearts,
Who can be little even in the light
Of thy meek holiness — while souls more great
Are left to wander in a starless night,
Praying unheard — and yet the hardest parts
Befit those best who best can cope with Fate.

IX.

Why should we ever weary of this life?
Our souls should widen ever, not contract,
Grow stronger, and not harder, in the strife,
Filling each moment with a noble act;
If we live thus, of vigor all compact,
Doing our duty to our fellow-men,
And striving rather to exalt our race
Than our poor selves, with earnest hand or pen
We shall erect our names a dwelling-place
Which not all ages shall cast down agen;
Offspring of Time shall then be born each hour,
Which, as of old, earth lovingly shall guard,
To live forever in youth's perfect flower,
And guide her future children Heavenward.

X.

GREEN MOUNTAINS.

Ye mountains, that far off lift up your heads,
Seen dimly through their canopies of blue,
The shade of my unrestful spirit sheds
Distance-created beauty over you;
I am not well content with this far view;
How may I know what foot of loved-one treads
Your rocks moss-grown and sun-dried torrent beds?
We should love all things better, if we knew

What claims the meanest have upon our hearts:
Perchance even now some eye, that would be bright
To meet my own, looks on your mist-robed forms;
Perchance your grandeur a deep joy imparts
To souls that have encircled mine with light —
O brother-heart, with thee my spirit warms!

XI.

My friend, adown Life's valley, hand in hand,
With grateful change of grave and merry speech
Or song, our hearts unlocking each to each,
We 'll journey onward to the silent land;
And when stern Death shall loose that loving band,
Taking in his cold hand a hand of ours,
The one shall strew the other's grave with flowers,
Nor shall his heart a moment be unmanned.
My friend and brother! if thou goest first,
Wilt thou no more re-visit me below?
Yea, when my heart seems happy, causelessly
And swells, not dreaming why, as it would burst
With joy unspeakable — my soul shall know
That thou, unseen, art bending over me.

XII.

VERSE cannot say how beautiful thou art,
How glorious the calmness of thine eyes,
Full of unconquerable energies,
Telling that thou hast acted well thy part.

No doubt or fear thy steady faith can start,
No thought of evil dare come nigh to thee,
Who hast the courage meek of purity,
The self-stayed greatness of a loving heart,
Strong with serene, enduring fortitude ;
Where'er thou art, that seems thy fitting place,
For not of forms, but Nature, art thou child ;
And lowest things put on a noble grace
When touched by ye, O patient, Ruth-like, mild
And spotless hands of earnest womanhood.

XIII.

THE soul would fain its loving kindness tell,
But custom hangs like lead upon the tongue ;
The heart is brimful, hollow crowds among,
When it finds one whose life and thought are well ;
Up to the eyes its gushing love doth swell,
The angel cometh and the waters move,
Yet it is fearful still to say " I love,"
And words come grating as a jangled bell.
O might we only speak but what we feel,
Might the tongue pay but what the heart doth owe,
Nor Heaven's great thunder, when, deep peal on peal,
It shakes the earth, could rouse our spirits so,
Or to the soul such majesty reveal,
As two short words half-spoken faint and low !

XIV.

I SAW a gate: a harsh voice spake and said,
" This is the gate of Life ; " above was writ,
" Leave hope behind, all ye who enter it ; "
Then shrank my heart within itself for dread ;
But, softer than the summer rain is shed,
Words dropt upon my soul, and they did say,
" Fear nothing, Faith shall save thee, watch and
        pray ! "
So, without fear I lifted up my head,
And lo ! that writing was not, one fair word
Was carven in its stead, and it was " Love."
Then rained once more those sweet tones from above
With healing on their wings : I humbly heard,
" I am the Life, ask and it shall be given !
I am the way, by me ye enter Heaven ! "

XV.

I WOULD not have this perfect love of ours
Grow from a single root, a single stem,
Bearing no goodly fruit, but only flowers
That idly hide Life's iron diadem :
It should grow alway like that Eastern tree
Whose limbs take root and spread forth constantly ;
That love for one. from which there doth not spring
Wide love for all, is but a worthless thing.

Not in another world, as poets prate,
Dwell we apart, above the tide of things,
High floating o'er earth's clouds on faery wings;
But our pure love doth ever elevate
Into a holy bond of brotherhood
All earthly things, making them pure and good.

XVI.

To the dark, narrow house where loved ones go,
Whence no steps outward turn, whose silent door
None but the sexton knocks at any more,
Are they not sometimes with us yet below?
The longings of the soul would tell us so;
Although, so pure and fine their being's essence,
Our bodily eyes are witless of their presence,
Yet not within the tomb their spirits glow,
Like wizard lamps pent up, but whensoever
With great thoughts worthy of their high behests
Our souls are filled, those bright ones with us be,
As, in the patriarch's tent, his angel guests; —
O let us live so worthily, that never
We may be far from that blest company.

XVII.

I FAIN would give to thee the loveliest things,
For lovely things belong to thee of right,
And thou hast been as peaceful to my sight,
As the still thoughts that summer twilight brings;

Beneath the shadow of thine angel wings
O let me live! O let me rest in thee,
Growing to thee more and more utterly,
Upbearing and upborn, till outward things
Are only as they share in thee a part!
Look kindly on me, let thy holy eyes
Bless me from the deep fulness of thy heart;
So shall my soul in its right strength arise.
And nevermore shall pine and shrink and start,
Safe-sheltered in thy full souled sympathies.

XVIII.

MUCH I had mused of Love, and in my soul
There was one chamber where I dared not look,
So much its dark and dreary voidness shook
My spirit, feeling that I was not whole:
All my deep longings flowed toward one goal
For long, long years, but were not answerèd,
Till Hope was drooping, Faith well-nigh stone-
        dead,
And I was still a blind, earth-delving mole;
Yet did I know that God was wise and good,
And would fulfil my being late or soon;
Nor was such thought in vain, for, seeing thee,
Great Love rose up, as, o'er a black pine wood,
Round, bright, and clear, upstarteth the full moon,
Filling my soul with glory utterly.

XIX.

SAYEST thou, most beautiful, that thou wilt wear
Flowers and leafy crowns when thou art old,
And that thy heart shall never grow so cold
But they shall love to wreathe thy silvered hair
And into age's snows the hope of spring-tide bear?
O, in thy childlike wisdom's moveless hold
Dwell ever! still the blessings manifold
Of purity, of peace, and untaught care
For other's hearts, around thy pathway shed,
And thou shalt have a crown of deathless flowers
To glorify and guard thy blessèd head
And give their freshness to thy life's last hours;
And, when the Bridegroom calleth, they shall be
A wedding-garment white as snow for thee.

XX.

POET! who sittest in thy pleasant room,
Warming thy heart with idle thoughts of love,
And of a holy life that leads above,
Striving to keep life's spring-flowers still in bloom,
And lingering to snuff their fresh perfume —
O, there were other duties meant for thee,
Than to sit down in peacefulness and Be!
O, there are brother-hearts that dwell in gloom,

Souls loathsome, foul, and black with daily sin,
So crusted o'er with baseness, that no ray
Of heaven's blessed light may enter in!
Come down, then, to the hot and dusty way,
And lead them back to hope and peace again —
For, save in Act, thy Love is all in vain.

XXI.

"NO MORE BUT SO?"

No more but so? Only with uncold looks,
And with a hand not laggard to clasp mine,
Think'st thou to pay what debt of love is thine?
No more but so? Like gushing water-brooks,
Freshening and making green the dimmest nooks
Of thy friend's soul thy kindliness should flow;
But, if 't is bounded by not saying "no,"
I can find more of friendship in my books,
All lifeless though they be, and more, far more
In every simplest moss, or flower, or tree;
Open to me thy heart of heart's deep core,
Or never say that I am dear to thee;
Call me not Friend, if thou keep close the door
That leads into thine inmost sympathy.

XXII.

TO A VOICE HEARD IN MOUNT AUBURN.

LIKE the low warblings of a leaf-hid bird,
Thy voice came to me through the screening trees,
Singing the simplest, long-known melodies;

I had no glimpse of thee, and yet I heard
And blest thee for each clearly-carolled word;
I longed to thank thee, and my heart would frame
Mary or Ruth, some sisterly, sweet name
For thee, yet could I not my lips have stirred;
I knew that thou wert lovely, that thine eyes
Were blue and downcast, and methought large tears,
Unknown to thee, up to their lids must rise
With half-sad memories of other years,
As to thyself alone thou sangest o'er
Words that to childhood seemed to say " No More!"

XXIII.

ON READING SPENSER AGAIN.

DEAR, gentle Spenser! thou my soul dost lead,
A little child again, through Fairy land,
By many a bower and stream of golden sand,
And many a sunny plain whose light doth breed
A sunshine in my happy heart, and feed
My fancy with sweet visions; I become
A knight, and with my charmèd arms would roam
To seek for fame in many a wondrous deed
Of high emprise — for I have seen the light
Of Una's angel's face, the golden hair
And backward eyes of startled Florimel;
And, for their holy sake I would outdare
A host of cruel Paynims in the fight,
Or Archimage and all the powers of Hell.

XXIV.

LIGHT of mine eyes! with thy so trusting look,
And thy sweet smile of charity and love,
That from a treasure well uplaid above,
And from a hope in Christ its blessing took;
Light of my heart! which, when it could not brook
The coldness of another's sympathy,
Finds ever a deep peace and stay in thee,
Warm as the sunshine of a mossy nook;
Light of my soul! who, by thy saintliness
And faith that acts itself in daily life,
Canst raise me above weakness, and canst bless
The hardest thraldom of my earthly strife —
I dare not say how much thou art to me
Even to myself — and O, far less to thee!

XXV.

SILENT as one who treads on new-fallen snow,
Love came upon me ere I was aware;
Not light of heart, for there was troublous care
Upon his eyelids, drooping them full low,
As with sad memory of a healèd woe;
The cold rain shivered in his g¹den hair,
As if an outcast lot had been his share,
And he seemed doubtful whither he should go:
Then he fell on my neck, and, in my breast
Hiding his face, awhile sobbed bitterly,

As half in grief to be so long distrest,
And half in joy at his security —
At last, uplooking from his place of rest,
His eyes shone blessedness and hope on me.

XXVI.

A GENTLENESS that grows of steady faith;
A joy that sheds its sunshine everywhere;
A humble strength and readiness to bear
Those burdens which strict duty ever lay'th
Upon our souls; — which unto sorrow saith,
" Here is no soil for thee to strike thy roots,
Here only grow those sweet and precious fruits
Which ripen for the soul that well obey'th;
A patience which the world can neither give
Nor take away; a courage strong and high,
That dares in simple usefulness to live,
And without one sad look behind to die
When that day comes; — these tell me that our love
Is building for itself a home above.

XXVII.

WHEN the glad soul is full to overflow,
Unto the tongue all power it denies,
And only trusts its secret to the eyes;
For, by an inborn wisdom, it doth know
There is no other eloquence but so;

And, when the tongue's weak utterance doth suffice,
Prisoned within the body's cell it lies,
Remembering in tears its exiled woe:
That word which all mankind so long to hear,
Which bears the spirit back to whence it came,
Maketh this sullen clay as crystal clear,
And will not be enclouded in a name;
It is a truth which we can feel and see,
But is as boundless as Eternity.

XXVIII.

TO THE EVENING-STAR.

WHEN we have once said lowly "Evening-Star!"
Words give no more — for, in thy silver pride,
Thou shinest as naught else can shine beside :
The thick smoke, coiling round the sooty bar
Forever, and the customed lamp-light mar
The stillness of my thought — seeing things glide
So samely : — then I ope my windows wide,
And gaze in peace to where thou shin'st afar ;
The wind that comes across the faint-white snow
So freshly, and the river dimly seen,
Seem like new things that never had been so
Before ; and thou art bright as thou hast been
Since thy white rays put sweetness in the eyes
Of the first souls that loved in Paradise.

XXIX.

READING.

As one who on some well-known landscape looks,
Be it alone, or with some dear friend nigh,
Each day beholdeth fresh variety,
New harmonies of hills, and trees, and brooks —
So it is with the worthiest choice of books,
And oftenest read: if thou no meaning spy,
Deem there is meaning wanting in thine eyes;
We are so lured from judgment by the crooks
And winding ways of covert fantasy,
Or turned unwittingly down beaten tracks
Of our foregone conclusions, that we see,
In our own want, the writer's misdeemed lacks:
It is with true books as with Nature, each
New day of living doth new insight teach.

XXX.

TO ——, AFTER A SNOW-STORM.

Blue as thine eyes the river gently flows
Between his banks, which, far as eye can see,
Are whiter than aught else on earth may be,
Save inmost thoughts that in my soul repose;
The trees, all crystalled by the melted snows,

Sparkle with gems and silver, such as we
In childhood saw 'mong groves of Faërie,
And the dear skies are sunny-blue as those;
Still as thy heart, when next mine own it lies
In love's full safety, is the bracing air;
The earth is all enwrapt with draperies
Snow-white as that pure love might choose to wear—
O for one moment's look into thine eyes,
To share the joy such scene would kindle there!

XXXI.

THROUGH suffering and sorrow thou hast past
To show us what a woman true may be:
They have not taken sympathy from thee,
Nor made thee any other than thou wast;
Save as some tree, which, in a sudden blast,
Sheddeth those blossoms, that are weakly grown,
Upon the air, but keepeth every one
Whose strength gives warrant of good fruit at last:
So thou hast shed some blooms of gayety,
But never one of steadfast cheerfulness;
Nor hath thy knowledge of adversity
Robbed thee of any faith in happiness,
But rather cleared thine inner eyes to see
How many simple ways there are to bless.

1840.

XXXII.

WHAT were I, Love, if I were stript of thee,
If thine eyes shut me out, whereby I live,
Thou, who unto my calmèd soul dost give
Knowledge, and truth, and holy Mystery,
Wherein Truth mainly lies for those who see
Beyond the earthly and the fugitive,
Who in the grandeur of the soul believe,
And only in the Infinite are free?
Without thee I were naked, bleak, and bare
As yon dead cedar on the sea-cliff's brow;
And nature's teachings, which come to me now
Common and beautiful as light and air,
Would be as fruitless as a stream which still
Slips through the wheel of some old ruined mill.

1841.

XXXIII.

IMPATIENCE AND REPROOF.

YES, I have felt a weariness of soul,
A shaking of my loveful faith in man,
Jostling with souls that ne'er beyond life's span
Have glimpsed, to whom this empty earth is goal
And starting-place, and death the dreadful whole;

But as, within the parlor's glare, at night,
Amid loud laugh, and converse vain and light,
Sudden without is heard the thunder's roll,
Deep-toned and infinite, with sad reproof, —
So, when my love and faith in man are shaken,
Great, inborn thoughts, that will not keep aloof,
Within my soul like those far thunders, waken,
Growing and growing, till its depths are dinned
With the sad sense of having deadly sinned.

  1841.

XXXIV.

REFORMERS.

IF ye have not the one great lesson learned,
Which grows in leaves, tides in the mighty sea,
And in the stars eternally hath burned,
That only full obedience is free, —
If ye in pride your true birthright have spurned,
Or, for a mess of pottage, beggarly
Have sold it, how, in Truth's name, have ye earned
The holy right to fight for Liberty?
Be free, and then our God will give a sword
Wherefor Orion's belt were not too bright;
There shall be power in your lightest word,
To make weak Falsehood, pierced with arrowy light,
Writhe, dying of her own most foul disease,
Within her churches and her palaces!

  1841.

XXXV.

THE FIERY TRIAL.

THE hungry flame hath never yet been hot
To him who won his name and crown of fire ;
But it doth ask a stronger soul and higher
To bear, not longing for a prouder lot,
Those martyrdoms whereof the world knows not, —
Hope sneaped with frosty scorn, the faith of youth
Wasted in seeming vain defence of Truth.
Greatness o'ertopt with baseness, and fame got
Too late : — Yet this most bitter task was meant
For those right worthy in such cause to plead,
And therefore God sent poets, men content
To live in humbleness and body's need.
If they may tread the path where Jesus went,
And sow one grain of Love's eternal seed.

   1841.

XXXVI.

GREAT Truths are portions of the soul of man ;
Great souls are portions of Eternity ;
Each drop of blood, that e'er through true heart ran
With lofty message, ran for thee and me ;
For God's law, since the starry song began,

Hath been, and still forevermore must be,
That every deed which shall outlast Time's span
Must goad the soul to be erect and free;
Slave is no word of deathless lineage sprung, —
Too many noble souls have thought and died,
Too many mighty poets lived and sung,
And our good Saxon, from lips purified
With martyr-fire, throughout the world hath rung
Too long to have God's holy cause denied.

1841.

XXXVII.

I ASK not for those thoughts, that sudden leap
From being's sea, like the isle-seeming Kraken,
With whose great rise the ocean all is shaken
And a heart-tremble quivers through the deep;
Give me that growth which some perchance deem
    sleep,
Wherewith the steadfast coral-stems uprise,
Which, by the toil of gathering energies,
Their upward way into clear sunshine keep,
Until, by Heaven's sweetest influences,
Slowly and slowly spreads a speck of green
Into a pleasant island in the seas,
Where, mid tall palms, the cane-roofed home is seen,
And wearied men shall sit at sunset's hour,
Hearing the leaves and loving God's dear power.

1841.

XXXVIII.

TO —— , ON HER BIRTH-DAY.

MAIDEN, when such a soul as thine is born,
The morning-stars their ancient music make,
And, joyful, once again their song awake,
Long silent now with melancholy scorn;
And thou, not mindless of so blest a morn,
By no least deed its harmony shalt break,
But shalt to that high chime thy footsteps take,
Through life's most darksome passes, unforlorn;
Therefore from thy pure faith thou shalt not fall,
Therefore shalt thou be ever fair and free,
And, in thine every motion, musical
As summer air, majestic as the sea,
A mystery to those who creep and crawl
Through Time, and part it from Eternity.

    1841.

XXXIX.

My Love, I have no fear that thou shouldst die;
Albeit I ask no fairer life than this,
Whose numbering-clock is still thy gentle kiss,
While Time and Peace with hands enlockèd fly, —
Yet care I not where in Eternity

We live and love, well knowing that there is
No backward step for those who feel the bliss
Of Faith as their most lofty yearnings high:
Love hath so purified my heart's strong core,
Meseems I scarcely should be startled, even,
To find, some morn, that thou hadst gone before;
Since, with thy love, this knowledge too was given,
Which each calm day doth · strengthen more and
   more,
That they who love are but one step from Heaven.

 1841.

XL.

I CANNOT think that thou shouldst pass away,
Whose life to mine is an eternal law,
A piece of nature that can have no flaw,
A new and certain sunrise every day;
But, if thou art to be another ray
About the Son of Life, and art to live
Free from all of thee that was fugitive,
The debt of Love I will more fully pay,
Not downcast with the thought of thee so high,
But rather raised to be a nobler man,
And more divine in my humanity,
As knowing that the waiting eyes which scan
My life are lighted by a purer being,
And ask meek, calm-browed deeds, with it agreeing.

 1841.

XLI.

THE HAVEN.

INTO the unruffled shelter of thy love
My bark leapt homeward from a rugged sea,
And furled its sails, and dropped right peacefully
Hope's anchor, quiet as a nested dove :
Thou givest me all that can the true soul move
To nobleness, — a clear simplicity,
That, in the humblest man to-day, can see
Theme for high rhyme as ever poet wove, —
A noiseless love that makes things common rare,
And custom-weary toil with heaven rife, —
A faith that finds great meanings everywhere,
That, to the soul's high level, raiseth life,
And puts in eyes, that could but dimly see,
The calm, vast presence of Eternity.

   1841.

XLII.

RESOLVE.

IN very truth, thou never art away,
Though miles between us cheat mine outward sense ;
For I do feel thee, both by night and day,
A hope fulfilled, a starry influence,

That floweth through my most forgetful deed,
And maketh crystal every part of me,
Sowing the common earth with golden seed,
Bright as if dropped down from the Galaxy:
In sooth, when we have seemed most far divided,
I inly felt we were most truly near,
For then a light from thy great love hath glided,
Through all that desert space, to give me cheer,
And, as light only where it strikes we see,
Men shall know this in my nobility.

    1841.

XLIII.

THERE never yet was flower fair in vain,
Let classic poets rhyme it as they will;
The seasons toil that it may blow again,
And summer's heart doth feel its every ill;
Nor is a true soul ever born for naught;
Wherever any such hath lived and died,
There hath been something for true freedom wrought,
Some bulwark levelled on the evil side:
Toil on, then, Greatness! thou art in the right,
However narrow souls may call thee wrong;
Be as thou wouldst be in thine own clear sight,
And so thou wilt in all the world's ere long;
For worldlings cannot, struggle as they may,
From man's great soul one great thought hide away.

XLIV.

SUB PONDERE CRESCIT.

THE hope of Truth grows stronger, day by day;
I hear the soul of Man around me waking,
Like a great sea, its frozen fetters breaking,
And flinging up to heaven its sunlit spray,
Tossing huge continents in scornful play,
And crushing them, with din of grinding thunder,
That makes old emptinesses stare in wonder;
The memory of a glory past away
Lingers in every heart, as, in the shell,
Ripples the bygone freedom of the sea,
And, every hour, new signs of promise tell
That the great soul shall once again be free,
For high, and yet more high, the murmurs swell
Of inward strife for truth and liberty.

1841.

XLV.

TO THE SPIRIT OF KEATS.

GREAT soul, thou sittest with me in my room,
Uplifting me with thy vast, quiet eyes,
On whose full orbs, with kindly lustre, lies
The twilight warmth of ruddy ember-gloom:
Thy clear, strong tones will oft bring sudden bloom

Of hope secure, to him who lonely cries,
Wrestling with the young poet's agonies,
Neglect and scorn, which seem a certain doom:
Yes! the few words which, like great thunder-drops,
Thy large heart down to earth shook doubtfully,
Thrilled by the inward lightning of its might,
Serene and pure, like gushing joy of light,
Shall track the eternal chords of Destiny,
After the moon-led pulse of ocean stops.

1841.

XLVI.

THE POET.

POET! thou art most wealthy, being poor;
For are not thine the only earthly ears
Made rich with golden music of the spheres?
Hast thou not snowy wings whereon to soar
Through the wide air of after and before,
And set thee high among thy crownèd peers?
Hath any man such joy as thy deep tears,
Or eyes like thine to pierce great nature's core?
Thou hast the fairy coin, which, in wrong hands,
Is merely stones and leaves, — in thine, true gold;
Thou art the very strength of all men's shields;
By divine right, art monarch of all lands;
And there is none but willing tribute yields,
Of worth too precious to be bought or sold.

1841.

XLVII.

Beloved, in the noisy city here,
The thought of thee can make all turmoil cease;
Around my spirit, folds thy spirit clear
Its still, soft arms, and circles it with peace;
There is no room for any doubt or fear
In souls so overfilled with love's increase,
There is no memory of the bygone year
But growth in heart's and spirit's perfect ease:
How hath our love, half nebulous at first,
Rounded itself into a full-orbed sun!
How have our lives and wills, (as haply erst
They were, ere this forgetfulness begun,)
Through all their earthly distantness outburst,
And melted, like two rays of light, in one!

1842.

XLVIII.

Full many noble friends my soul hath known,
Women and men, who in my memory
Have sown such beauty as can never die;
And many times, when I seem all alone,
Within my heart I call up, one by one,

The joys I shared with them, the unlaced hours
Of laughing thoughts, that came and went like flowers,
Or higher argument, Apollo's own :
Those listening eyes that gave nobility
To humblest verses writ and read for love,
Those burning words of high democracy,
Those doubts that through the vague abyss would rove
And lean o'er chasms that took away the breath, —
When I forget them, may it be in death !

    1842.

XLIX.

How oft do I live o'er that blissful time
When first I found thy love within my breast,
Like the first violet in April's prime,
Born a full flower, more fair than all the rest,
And richer with the early dew of rhyme !
Till then, I felt my heart was but a guest
In the broad world, but now there is no clime
Where it as rightful sovereign may not rest :
Wherever Nature even a weed doth plant,
There it the fulness of delight may win ;
No dead or living thing will let it want,
None but whose heart will freely take it in ;
For Love hath made it now wise Nature's child,
And from her arms it cannot be exiled.

    1842.

L.

SLOW-OPENING flower of the summer morn, —
Blithe quietness of sun-delighted dew, —
Green inland oceans of unrippling corn, —
Deep thoughtfulness of never-wrinkled blue,
Whose high, eternal silence seemeth born
For the lone moon and stars to wander through, —
Sunset, — and all the wreaths by Nature worn,
And momently thrown by for beauties new, —
My heart grows fragrant while on you I look,
And murmurs to itself, and feels at ease,
And trembles, like a sunny birch-tree shook
In rustling sparkles by a warm noon-breeze ;
Yet, when I see my Love, my heart runs o'er
With sympathies and strengths undreamed before.

1842.

LI.

TO M. O. S.

MARY, since first I knew thee, to this hour,
My love hath deepened, with my wiser sense
Of what in Woman is to reverence ;
Thy clear heart, fresh as e'er was forest-flower,
Still opens more to me its beauteous dower ; —
But let praise hush, — Love asks no evidence
To prove itself well-placed ; we know not whence
It gleans the straws that thatch its humble bower :

We can but say we found it in the heart,
Spring of all sweetest thoughts, arch-foe of blame,
Sower of flowers in the dusty mart,
Pure vestal of the poet's holy flame, —
This is enough, and we have done our part
If we but keep it spotless as it came.

    1842.

LII.

OUR love is not a fading, earthly flower;
Its wingèd seed dropt down from Paradise,
And, nurst by day and night, by sun and shower,
Doth momently to fresher beauty rise:
To us the leafless autumn is not bare,
Nor winter's rattling boughs lack lusty green.
Our summer hearts make summer's fulness, where
No leaf, or bud, or blossom may be seen:
For nature's life in love's deep life doth lie,
Love, — whose forgetfulness is beauty's death,
Whose mystic key these cells of Thou and I
Into the infinite freedom openeth,
And makes the body's dark and narrow grate
The wide-flung leaves of Heaven's palace-gate.

    1842.

LIII.

THANKFULNESS.

THERE is no thankfulness more deep than this, —
To love and love with ever-glad increase,
To nestle in the heart with fluttering bliss
And think that now is the full tide of peace;

Yet still to find, with each sun-circled hour,
A higher right to love, unhoped before,
A fuller insight, a serener power,
That widens down the soul's unfathomed core:
To feel that we are blest is thankfulness,
And thereby with exulting faith to know
That every human heart its kind must bless
With love, which, garnered up, rusts into woe,
But, freely given, always turns again,
And, for our flowers, brings us ripened grain.

1842.

LIV.

IN ABSENCE.

THESE rugged, wintry days I scarce could bear,
Did I not know, that, in the early spring,
When wild March winds upon their errands sing,
Thou wouldst return, bursting on this still air,
Like those same winds, when, startled from their lair,
They hunt up violets, and free swift brooks
From icy cares, even as thy clear looks
Bid my heart bloom, and sing, and break all care:
When drops with welcome rain the April day,
My flowers shall find their April in thine eyes,
Save there the rain in dreamy clouds doth stay,
As loath to fall out of those happy skies;
Yet sure, my love, thou art most like to May,
That comes with steady sun when April dies.

1843.

LV.

WENDELL PHILLIPS

HE stood upon the world's broad threshold; wide
The din of battle and of slaughter rose;
He saw God stand upon the weaker side,
That sank in seeming loss before its foes;
Many there were who made great haste and sold
Unto the cunning enemies their swords;
He scorned their gifts of fame, and power and gold,
And, underneath their soft and flowery words,
Heard the cold serpent hiss; therefore he went
And humbly joined him to the weaker part,
Fanatic named, and fool, yet well content
So he could be the nearer to God's heart
And feel its solemn pulses sending blood
Through all the wide-spread veins of endless good.

LVI.

THE STREET.

THEY pass me by like shadows, crowds on crowds,
Dim ghosts of men, that hover to and fro,
Hugging their bodies around them, like thin shrouds
Wherein their souls were buried long ago:
They trampled on their youth, and faith, and love,

They cast their hope of human-kind away,
With Heaven's clear messages they madly strove.
And conquered, — and their spirits turned to clay:
Lo! how they wander round the world, their grave,
Whose ever-gaping maw by such is fed,
Gibbering at living men, and idly rave,
"We, only, truly live, but ye are dead."
Alas! poor fools, the anointed eye may trace
A dead soul's epitaph in every face!

LVII.

I GRIEVE not that ripe Knowledge takes away
The charm that Nature to my childhood wore,
For, with that insight, cometh, day by day,
A greater bliss than wonder was before;
The real doth not clip the poet's wings, —
To win the secret of a weed's plain heart
Reveals some clew to spiritual things,
And stumbling guess becomes firm-footed art:
Flowers are not flowers unto the poet's eyes,
Their beauty thrills him by an inward sense;
He knows that outward seemings are but lies,
Or, at the most, but earthly shadows, whence
The soul that looks within for truth may guess
The presence of some wondrous heavenliness.

LVIII.

YE who behold the body of my thought,
Whose minds can surfeit on an outward grace,
Ye learn but half the lesson that is taught,
Looking no deeper down than Nature's face;

Two meanings have our lightest fantasies,
One of the flesh, and of the spirit one,
And he who skips the latter only sees
The painter's colors and the sculptor's stone:
Unfathomably deep are all good things,
Each day therefrom the soul may drink its fill,
And straight a clearer truth to being springs,
The self-renewing fount o'errunneth still;
For the unconscious poet can but write
What is foretold him by the Infinite.

LIX.

O, HAPPY childhood! dear, unthoughtful years
When life flowed onward like a rover wind,
Why did I leave your peace of heart behind
To plunge me in this sea of doubts and fears?
Down, foolish sigh! have not my manhood's tears
Washed off the scales that made my nature blind,
Letting Truth's growing light sure passage find
Into my soul, where now the sky half-clears?
Thank God that I am numbered now with men,
That there are hearts that need my love and me,
That I have sorrows now to make me ken
My strength and weakness, and my right to be
Brother to those, the outcast and the poor,
Driven back to darkness from the world's proud door!

LX.

ON MY TWENTY-FOURTH BIRTH-DAY, FEBRUARY 22, 1843.

Now have I quite passed by that cloudy If
That darkened the wild hope of boyish days,
When first I launched my slender-sided skiff
Upon the wide sea's dim, unsounded ways;
Now doth Love's sun my soul with splendor fill,
And Hope hath struggled upward into Power,
Soft Wish is hardened into sinewy Will,
And Longing into Certainty doth tower:
The love of beauty knoweth no despair;
My heart would break, if I should dare to doubt,
That from the Wrong, which makes its dragon's lair
Here on the Earth, fair Truth shall wander out,
Teaching mankind, that Freedom's held in fee
Only by those who labor to set free.

LXI.

TO J. R. GIDDINGS.

GIDDINGS, far rougher names than thine have grown
Smoother than honey on the lips of men;
And thou shalt aye be honorably known,
As one who bravely used his tongue and pen,

As best befits a freeman, — even for those,
To whom our Law's unblushing front denies
A right to plead against the life-long woes
Which are the Negro's glimpse of Freedom's skies:
Fear nothing and hope all things, as the Right
Alone may do securely; every hour
The thrones of Ignorance and ancient Night
Lose somewhat of their long-usurpèd power,
And Freedom's lightest word can make them shiver
With a base dread that clings to them forever.

SONNETS ON NAMES.

I.

EDITH.

A LILY with its frail cup filled with dew,
Down-bending modestly, snow-white and pale,
Shedding faint fragrance round its native vale,
Minds me of thee, Sweet Edith, mild and true,
And of thy eyes so innocent and blue.
Thy heart is fearful as a startled hare,
Yet hath in it a fortitude to bear
For Love's sake, and a gentle faith which grew
Of Love: need of a stay whereon to lean,
Felt in thyself, hath taught thee to uphold
And comfort others, and to give, unseen,
The kindness thy still love cannot withhold:
Maiden, I would my sister thou hadst been,
That round thee I my guarding arms might fold.

II.

ROSE.

My ever-lightsome, ever-laughing Rose,
Who always speakest first and thinkest last,
Thy full voice is as clear as bugle-blast;
Right from the ear down to the heart it goes
And says " I 'm beautiful! as who but knows?"
Thy name reminds me of old romping days,
Of kisses stolen in dark passage-ways,
Or in the parlor, if the mother-nose
Gave sign of drowsy watch.   I wonder where
Are gone thy tokens, given with a glance
So full of everlasting love till morrow,
Or a day's endless grieving for the dance
Last night denied, backed with a lock of hair,
That spake of broken hearts and deadly sorrow.

III.

MARY.

Dark hair, dark eyes — not too dark to be deep
And full of feeling, yet enough to glow
With fire when angered; feelings never slow,
But which seem rather watching to forthleap
From her full breast; a gently-flowing sweep
Of words in common talk, a torrent-rush,
Whenever through her soul swift feelings gush,
A heart less ready to be gay than weep,

Yet cheerful ever; a calm matron-smile,
That bids God bless you; a chaste simpleness,
With somewhat, too, of " proper pride," in dress ; —
This portrait to my mind's eye came, the while
I thought of thee, the well-grown woman Mary,
Whilome a gold-haired, laughing little fairy.

IV.

CAROLINE.

A STAIDNESS sobers o'er her pretty face,
Which something but ill-hidden in her eyes,
And a quaint look about her lips denies ;
A lingering love of girlhood you can trace
In her checked laugh and half-restrainèd pace ;
And, when she bears herself most womanly,
It seems as if a watchful mother's eye
Kept down with sobering glance her childish grace :
Yet oftentimes her nature gushes free
As water long held back by little hands,
Within a pump, and let forth suddenly,
Until, her task remembering, she stands
A moment silent, smiling doubtfully,
Then laughs aloud and scorns her hated bands.

V.

ANNE.

THERE is a pensiveness in quiet Anne,
A mournful drooping of the full gray eye,
As if she had shook hands with misery,

And known some care since her short life began;
Her cheek is seriously pale, nigh wan,
And, though of cheerfulness there is no lack,
You feel as if she must be drest in black;
Yet is she not of those who, all they can,
Strive to be gay, and striving, seem most sad —
Hers is not grief, but silent soberness;
You would be startled if you saw her glad,
And startled if you saw her weep, no less;
She walks through life, as, on the Sabbath day,
She decorously glides to church to pray.

L'ENVOI.

TO M. W.

WHETHER my heart hath wiser grown or not,
In these three years, since I to thee inscribed,
Mine own betrothed, the firstlings of my muse, —
Poor windfalls of unripe experience,
Young buds plucked hastily by childish hands
Not patient to await more full-blown flowers, —
At least it hath seen more of life and men,
And pondered more, and grown a shade more sad;
Yet with no loss of hope or settled trust
In the benignness of that Providence,
Which shapes from out our elements awry
The grace and order that we wonder at,

The mystic harmony of right and wrong,
Both working out His wisdom and our good:
A trust, Belovèd, chiefly learned of thee,
Who hast that gift of patient tenderness,
The instinctive wisdom of a woman's heart,
Which, seeing Right, can yet forgive the Wrong,
And, strong itself to comfort and sustain,
Yet leans with full-confiding piety
On the great Spirit that encircles all.

Less of that feeling, which the world calls love,
Thou findest in my verse, but haply more
Of a more precious virtue, born of that,
The love of God, of Freedom, and of Man.
Thou knowest well what these three years have been,
How we have filled and graced each other's hearts,
And every day grown fuller of that bliss,
Which, even at first seemed more than we could bear,
And thou, meantime, unchanged, except it be
That thy large heart is larger, and thine eyes
Of palest blue, more tender with the lore
Which taught me first how good it was to love;
And, if thy blessed name occur less oft,
Yet thou canst see the shadow of thy soul
In all my song, and art well-pleased to feel
That I could ne'er be rightly true to thee,
If I were recreant to higher aims.
Thou didst not grant to me so rich a fief
As thy full love, on any harder tenure
Than that of rendering thee a single heart;

And I do service for thy queenly gift
Then best, when I obey my soul, and tread
In reverence the path she beckons me.

'T were joy enough, — if I could think that life
Were but a barren struggle after joy, —
To live, and love, and never look beyond
The fair horizon of thy bounteous heart,
Whose sunny circle stretches wide enough
For me to find a heaped contentment in ;
To do naught else but garner every hour
My golden harvest of sweet memories,
And count my boundless revenues of smiles
And happy looks, and words so kind and gentle
That each doth seem the first to give thy heart, —
Content to let my waveless soul flow on,
Reflecting but the spring-time on its brink,
And thy clear spirit bending like a sky
O'er it, — secure that from thy virgin hands
My brows should never lack their dearest wreath :
But life hath nobler destinies than this,
Which but to strive for is reward enough,
Which to attain is all earth gives of peace.
Thou art not of those niggard souls, who deem
That Poesy is but to jingle words,
To string sweet sorrows for apologies
To hide the bareness of unfurnished hearts,
To prate about the surfaces of things,
And make more threadbare what was quite worn out :
Our common thoughts are deepest, and to give
Such beauteous tones to these, as needs must take

Men's hearts their captives to the end of time,
So that who hath not the choice gift of words
Takes these into his soul, as welcome friends,
To make sweet music of his joys and woes,
And be all Beauty's swift interpreters,
Links of bright gold 'twixt Nature and his heart.
This is the errand high of Poesy.
The day has long gone by wherein 't was thought
That men were greater poets, inasmuch
As they were more unlike their fellow-men:
The poet sees beyond, but dwells among,
The wearing turmoil of our work-day life;
His heart not differs from another heart,
But rather in itself enfolds the whole
Felt by the hearts about him, high or low,
Hath deeper sympathies and clearer sight
And is more like a human heart than all;
His larger portion is but harmony
Of heart, the all-potent alchemy that turns
The humblest things to golden inspiration;
A loving eye's unmatchèd sovereignty;
A self-sustained, enduring humbleness;
A reverence for woman; a deep faith
In gentleness, as strength's least doubtful proof;
And an electric sympathy with love,
Heaven's first great message to all noble souls.

But, if the poet's duty be to tell
His fellow-men their beauty and their strength,
And show them the deep meaning of their souls,
He also is ordained to higher things;

He must reflect his race's struggling heart,
And shape the crude conceptions of his age.
They tell us that our land was made for song,
With its huge rivers and sky-piercing peaks,
Its sea-like lakes and mighty cataracts,
Its forests vast and hoar, and prairies wide,
And mounds that tell of wondrous tribes extinct;
But Poesy springs not from rocks and woods;
Her womb and cradle are the human heart,
And she can find a nobler theme for song
In the most loathsome man that blasts the sight,
Than in the broad expanse of sea and shore
Between the frozen deserts of the poles.
All nations have their message from on high,
Each the messiah of some central thought,
For the fulfilment and delight of Man:
One has to teach that labor is divine;
Another, Freedom; and another, Mind;
And all, that God is open-eyed and just,
The happy centre and calm heart of all.

Are, then, our woods, our mountains, and our
     streams,
Needful to teach our poets how to sing?
O, maiden rare, far other thoughts were ours,
When we have sat by ocean's foaming marge,
And watched the waves leap roaring on the rocks,
Than young Leander and his Hero had,
Gazing from Sestos to the other shore.
The moon looks down and ocean worships her,
Stars rise and set, and seasons come and go

Even as they did in Homer's elder time,
But we behold them not with Grecian eyes:
Then they were types of beauty and of strength,
But now of freedom, unconfined and pure,
Subject alone to Order's higher law.
What cares the Russian serf or Southern slave,
Though we should speak as man spake never yet
Of gleaming Hudson's broad magnificence,
Or green Niagara's never-ending roar ?
Our country hath a gospel of her own
To preach and practise before all the world, —
The freedom and divinity of man,
The glorious claims of human brotherhood, —
Which to pay nobly, as a freeman should,
Gains the sole wealth that will not fly away, —
And the soul's fealty to none but God.
These are realities, which make the shows
Of outward Nature, be they ne'er so grand,
Seem small, and worthless, and contemptible.
These are the mountain-summits for our bards,
Which stretch far upward into heaven itself,
And give such wide-spread and exulting view
Of hope, and faith, and onward destiny,
That shrunk Parnassus to a molehill dwindles.
Our new Atlantis, like a morning-star,
Silvers the murk face of slow-yielding Night,
The herald of a fuller truth than yet
Hath gleamed upon the upraised face of Man
Since the earth glittered in her stainless prime, —
Of a more glorious sunrise than of old
Drew wondrous melodies from Memnon huge,

Yea, draws them still, though now he sits waist-deep
In the engulfing flood of whirling sand,
And looks across the wastes of endless gray,
Sole wreck, where once his hundred-gated Thebes
Pained with her mighty hum the calm, blue heaven:
Shall the dull stone pay grateful orisons,
And we till noonday bar the splendor out,
Lest it reproach and chide our sluggard hearts,
Warm-nestled in the down of Prejudice,
And be content, though clad with angel-wings,
Close-clipt, to hop about from perch to perch,
In paltry cages of dead men's dead thoughts?
O, rather, like the sky-lark, soar and sing,
And let our gushing songs befit the dawn
And sunrise, and the yet unshaken dew
Brimming the chalice of each full-blown hope,
Whose blithe front turns to greet the growing day!
Never had poets such high call before,
Never can poets hope for higher one,
And, if they be but faithful to their trust,
Earth will remember them with love and joy,
And, O, far better, God will not forget.
For he who settles Freedom's principles
Writes the death-warrant of all tyranny;
Who speaks the truth stabs Falsehood to the heart,
And his mere word makes despots tremble more
Than ever Brutus with his dagger could.
Wait for no hints from waterfalls or woods,
Nor dream that tales of red men, brute and fierce,
Repay the finding of this Western World,
Or needed half the globe to give them birth:

Spirit supreme of Freedom! not for this
Did great Columbus tame his eagle soul
To jostle with the daws that perch in courts;
Not for this, friendless, on an unknown sea,
Coping with mad waves and more mutinous spirits,
Battled he with the dreadful ache at heart
Which tempts, with devilish subtleties of doubt,
The hermit of that loneliest solitude,
The silent desert of a great New Thought;
Though loud Niagara were to-day struck dumb,
Yet would this cataract of boiling life
Rush plunging on and on to endless deeps,
And utter thunder till the world shall cease, —
A thunder worthy of the poet's song,
And which alone can fill it with true life.
The high evangel to our country granted
Could make apostles, yea, with tongues of fire,
Of hearts half-darkened back again to clay!
'T is the soul only that is national,
And he who pays true loyalty to that
Alone can claim the wreath of patriotism.

Belovèd! if I wander far and oft
From that which I believe, and feel, and know,
Thou wilt forgive, not with a sorrowing heart,
But with a strengthened hope of better things;
Knowing that I, though often blind and false
To those I love, and, O, more false than all
Unto myself, have been most true to thee,
And that whoso in one thing hath been true

Can be as true in all.   Therefore thy hope
May yet not prove unfruitful, and thy love
Meet, day by day, with less unworthy thanks,
Whether, as now, we journey hand in hand
Or, parted in the body, yet are one
In spirit and the love of holy things.